The Internet Guide
for Writers

Books to change your life and work.
Accessible, easy to read and easy to act on –
Other titles in the **How To** series include:

The Writer's Guide to Research
*An invaluable guide to gathering material for features, novels
and non-fiction books*

Writer's Guide to Copyright and Law
Get you full financial reward and steer clear of legal pitfalls

Writing for Publication
What to write; how to write it; where and how to sell it

Publishing a Book
How to publish your own work and make a profit

Awaken the Writer Within
How to discover and release your true writer's voice

The **How To** series now contains
around 200 titles in the following categories:

Business & Management
Career Choices
Career Development
Computers & the Net
Creative Writing
Home & Family
Living & Working Abroad
Personal Development
Personal Finance
Self-Employment & Small Business
Study Skills & Student Guides

For full details, please send for a free copy
of the latest catalogue to:

How To Books
3 Newtec Place, Magdalen Road
Oxford OX4 1RE, United Kingdom
e-mail: info@howtobooks.co.uk
http://www.howtobooks.co.uk

The Internet Guide for Writers

*Use the internet for writing,
research and information*

MALCOLM CHISHOLM

How To Books

Published by How To Books Ltd,
3 Newtec Place, Magdalen Road,
Oxford OX4 1RE, United Kingdom.
Tel: (01865) 793806. Fax: (01865) 248780.
email: info@howtobooks.co.uk
http://www.howtobooks.co.uk

First edition 2001

British Library Cataloguing in Publication Data.
A catalogue record for this book is available from
the British Library.

Edited by Francesca Mitchell
Cover design by Shireen Nathoo Design
Cover image by PhotoDisc

Produced for How To Books by Deer Park Productions
Typeset by Kestrel Data, Exeter
Printed and bound by Cromwell Press Ltd, Trowbridge, Wiltshire

NOTE: The material contained in this book is set out in good
faith for general guidance and no liability can be accepted
for loss or expense incurred as a result of relying in particular
circumstances on statements made in the book. Laws and
regulations are complex and liable to change, and readers should
check the current position with the relevant authorities before
making personal arrangements.

Contents

Acknowledgements

BBC World Service screen shots, page 77, copyright BBC World Service.

Infoseek screen shots, pages 38 and 39, reprinted by permission. Disney Enterprises, Inc. trademarks may be registered in certain jurisdictions.

Lycos screen shot, page 40, © Lycos Europe, 2000.

The Times screen shots, pages 68 and 69, copyright © Times Newspapers Limited, London, 2000.

WinZip screen shots, page 125, copyright 1991–2000, WinZip Computing, Inc. and reproduced with their permission. Illustrations copyright 1991–2000, WinZip Computing Inc. WinZip(R) is a registered trademark of WinZip Computing, Inc. WinZip screen images reproduced with permission of WinZip Computing, Inc.

Illustrations copyright Dolphin Software Solutions. The Working Writer is a registered trademark of Dolphin Software Solutions.

Thank you to Andrew Chisholm and John Poole for their help with this book.

Introduction

'THE INTERNET? I'M A WRITER, SO WHAT'S IN IT FOR ME?'

Where do you go when you want to research something? Who do you turn to? Your local library, perhaps? Could you pop round to the local university? Do you write to an expert and hope he can help? Why not telephone someone to discuss the topic? These all take time and effort. Does the library have the book in stock or was your journey wasted? How far away is the local university? How long does the letter take to be delivered? Where is the person you want to talk to?

The Internet is all of these things: library, mail company, discussion medium, videophone system. To the writer it is a library of pages of information, all of which are grouped into **Web sites**. The pages are cross-referenced so that the reader can jump immediately to other pages, which are judged by the providers to be of relevance to the subject being researched. There are hundreds of millions of pages on every subject imaginable.

Universities were among the first organisations to use the Internet and they have embraced it enthusiastically. They have enormous resources devoted to academic and research material. Newspapers provide access to their archives. Governments keep us informed of their latest developments (or propaganda). Other organisations provide information, maybe about their history, their *raison d'être* or products that they can supply. Individuals, both experts and enthusiasts, display information on subjects close to their hearts.

The most amazing thing of all is that this information is there for the taking. No need to ask, just take it. If the providers didn't want you to have it, they wouldn't put it there in the first place, and what is more, IT IS USUALLY FREE!

Whatever it is that you want to find out, you may be sure that it is only a mouse-click away on the **World Wide Web** . . .

Notes:

Bold type indicates that a word or phrase is included in the Glossary at the end of the book.

Italic type indicates a Web address, e.g. *www.bbc.co.uk*.

Most **web addresses** you will find are in the form *http://www.mywebaddress.co.uk* and the letters 'http' have been omitted. However, some addresses do not include the 'www', in which case the 'http://' is included. When entering a web address into a **web browser** the 'http://' part may always be left out.

The Internet and its associated technology is developing so fast that this book is a snapshot of how things stand at the time of writing. Always be prepared for new advances to take over and improve on what is mentioned here. Much of the information is in appendices to enable it to be as up to date as possible.

USING YOUR MOUSE

'Click' means point at an object or image on the screen and press the left or normal mouse button once.

'Double click' means point at an object and click twice in quick succession.

'Right click' means point at an object and press the right or alternative mouse button.

'Drag' or 'Drag and drop' means point at an object, hold down the left or normal button and keep it pressed while moving the pointer to another location on the screen, then release the button.

If you are left-handed, you may well have reversed the button operations, so that the right button is normal and the left button is the alternative button. If you are using an Apple Macintosh computer, you will only have one button on your mouse.

1

Setting Up

WHAT IS THE INTERNET?

The **Internet** is a network of computers connected all around the world. It started in America and is still very much US-led, but its tentacles now reach into almost every country in the world, including the north and south poles.

The computers that are connected range from large government, university and commercial **mainframes** to individuals' **PCs**. Some are connected permanently while others connect to the Internet (or go **on-line**) temporarily to look for information then drop the connection (go **off-line**) when they have finished. There are hundreds of millions of them and anyone can take part. Some would say that the Internet is creating the biggest social change since the Industrial Revolution.

It is certainly revolutionising the world of the writer. **Electronic mail, desktop conferencing** and the enormous information resources of the **World Wide Web** covering every subject imaginable are all at the writer's fingertips. As the advertising copywriter could have said, 'Every writer should have it'.

WHAT YOU NEED

The Internet is accessible to anyone who owns a computer. In addition, you need a telephone line with a modern socket, a **modem** (which connects your computer to the telephone system via the socket), and a **service provider** (someone to provide you with your Internet service). There are alternatives to the modem for intensive users listed at the end of this chapter.

Your computer

The computer does not have to be all-singing-all-dancing. Indeed, if you only want to use it for the Internet and word processing then a modest computer will do nicely. In PC terms (PC meaning IBM-compatible personal computer) a **Pentium 75** with **32 mega**

bytes (32 million bytes) of **RAM** memory will do quite well. However, if you want to do much more than **surf the web**, send **electronic mail**, word processing, and other office applications then you should be looking for something more powerful.

Speak to your local computer dealers and make enquiries of your nearest technical college. Compare their answers and beware of anyone who suggests that you buy a computer costing more than £800. Many computers sales people are on commission!

There are many second-hand computers for sale. Have a look at them, but remember to take someone who knows about these things along with you. Make sure that you see it working and doing what you want it to do before you part with your cash.

The modem

The **modem** allows your computer to communicate over the telephone line with the **Internet Service Provider**, or **ISP** (see below). If the computer does not have a modem with it, then you will need to buy one – the faster, the better. Modem speed is measured in 'bits per second'. That is the speed at which the modem can send and receive the **data**. The absolute minimum speed to consider is 28,800 (or 28.8K), and the usual speed is 56,000 (56K). This is currently the fastest you can buy and it will make a real difference to the speed at which data is received. This can be important as you may well be paying for the time you spend connected to the Internet by the telephone system.

Modems can be fitted internally in your computer or connected externally, plugged into a **serial port** socket on the back. Internal modems take up no extra space on your desk, but external modems have the advantage of lights on the front which can tell you when you are connected and an on/off switch that you can use if it doesn't disconnect when it should.

Look in the section 'Do I have to use the phone?' later in this chapter for more details on how to access the Internet.

Service Providers

The **Internet Service Provider (ISP)** or **Internet Access Provider (IAP)** provides you, via your modem and telephone line, with the connection to the Internet. Both will allow you to dial a local number and connect to the Internet. They may or (more frequently) may not charge you for the service, but in either case you will be able to **log in** to their computers and from there get access to anywhere in the world at (usually) no extra charge.

The difference between them is that an **Internet Access Provider** will simply enable you to gain access to the Internet, while the **Internet Service Provider** will supply you with extra services. These may include:

- news feeds

- information services

- communications facilities

- interactive games

- specialist 'themed' services

- search facilities

- links to commercial Web sites

- customised start-up pages

- your own web space in which you can put information for others to see.

Fig. 1.   The Freeserve **home page**. Note the popular magazine-style information layout.

In either case you will probably find that you are confronted by advertising, which helps to pay for the service.

Why should I pay for the service?

All service providers will supply you with access to the **World Wide Web** and will allow you one or more **email** addresses.

You need to decide whether it is worth your while to pay for the service. Free services are springing up all the time. They are paid for by a combination of the telephone companies giving them a proportion of what you pay for the calls and by advertising. Paid-for service costs anywhere from £5 to £15 per month. There are advantages and disadvantages to both:

	Paid-for services	**Free services**
Subscription cost	£5–£15 per month	Free
Phone time costs	Can include free evening and/or weekend time. Some have permanent free phone access but may charge for time logged on.	Usually local call rate
Helpdesk charges	Free or local call rate	Premium call rate
Speed of service*	Tends to be faster	Tends to be slower, especially at popular times
Availability*	Tends to be better	Tends to be poorer
Content	Often includes material for subscribers only	Many commercial and advertising links

Note that the telephone charge for calling the service provider to make the Internet connection must be added to any on-line charges.

*A 'speed and availability' league table is published monthly in *Internet* magazine. Positions in this table can vary considerably from month to month so a six-month average is also published.

You may wish to check this and look at the services provided before you make your choice.

What about telephone call charges?
Normally you will pay for a local telephone call to make and maintain the connection while you are on-line. This is in addition to any fees charged by the ISP. However, some ISPs are now including **unmetered** calls to their services, but charge a flat fee for their service. At the time of writing, AOL charges £9.99 per month plus 1p per minute on-line time charge (the telephone call costs nothing) or £14.99 per month for unlimited free access. LineOne charges £9.99 through your telephone bill and gives free evening and weekend access, but charges 1p per minute at other times.

Other 'free' access offers are conditional on you using another service. Freeserve customers who use a BT telephone line can have free access, provided that they spend a minimum of £10 on voice telephone calls switched through the Energis phone company. Before you sign up, check the figures as deals change very quickly in order to respond to competitors' offers.

So the competition is fierce and the situation is changing rapidly. Look out for advertisements in the Internet magazines and newspapers. A criticism of services that include free calls is that they are often difficult to connect because of their popularity. Some attempts at supplying totally free access have collapsed spectacularly. For the time being, do not rely on totally 'free' services. Expect to pay something.

Before you sign up to a service that charges a monthly fee, try a service provider which makes no charge but where you pay the call charges. See how much you are paying for your Internet access calls. It may well be less than the monthly charge. Just ask your phone company to give you fully itemised bills so that you can add up the total cost of your Internet calls.

CONNECTING UP

The process of getting connected to an internet service provider has been simplified enormously. In many cases, a new computer will already be set up for a service provider when it is delivered. This is fine if you are happy to use the provider whose service has been set up on your machine. If you want to use any other provider or you do not have one set up already, you will see them advertised in newspapers, magazines and on television. Many ISPs supply free or cheap **CD-ROMs** to start you off.

Quite a few organisations now provide on-line services linked to the ISP function. In particular, look for supermarkets, banks, gas and electricity companies, stockbrokers and others. Free ISPs also like to give their sites a magazine-like flavour, to make them more popular. Look at their sites to see which ones appeal to you. To get started, there are some contact points in the ISP appendix at the end of the book.

Do I have to use the phone?

Normally a domestic user or small business would use the telephone line to connect to an ISP, but there are various types of service available:

- Ordinary telephone calls to a local rate number such as 0845 . . .

- **ISDN** – a high-speed digital service with a higher line rental and local call charges.

- **ADSL** – started September 2000. Your computer is on-line permanently and you can make phone calls at the same time as you use the Internet.

Ordinary phone lines

Your modem will be programmed to call a fixed number. You may be charged at local call rates according to the time of day. You can reduce the cost of these calls by using a low-cost telephone carrier and by calling only at cheap-rate times. You may wish to make your ISP number a 'Friends and Family' number. Some ISPs give you free telephone call access and charge you for the time you are connected to them or you may pay a fixed monthly or annual fee by direct debit.

The data will come down the phone line at the fastest speed your modem can manage, subject to a maximum speed of roughly 44,000 bits per second (around 4,400 characters per second). This figure is called the **baud rate** or **data transfer rate**.

If your telephone service is provided by a cable television company you could use a **cable modem**, which will give you a faster baud rate. You cannot make other calls while you are connected to the Internet.

ISDN lines

ISDN lines are high-speed digital phone lines, mainly used by businesses and others with large amounts of data to transfer. This service allows speeds of up to 128,000 bits per second (bps). They are more expensive to rent but call charges are the same as ordinary telephone lines. The modem is replaced by an ISDN interface card inside the computer. Connection to the ISP takes under a second and is very reliable. You have access to two lines, so one can make and receive telephone calls while the other is in use for the Internet.

ADSL (Asymmetric Digital Subscriber Line)

ADSL is a brand new technology. It is a means of getting Internet access by piggy-backing high-speed data transfer on the existing telephone line. It enables users to stay on-line permanently and also make telephone calls. Data transfer rates of up to 2 Mbps (2 *mega*-bits per second or 200,000 characters per second) are possible. A monthly fee of around £40 is paid for the Internet service, but you are permanently connected.

Other telephone calls are made and charged for as normal, and they will not interfere with your Internet use. The monthly fee includes the ADSL modem. ADSL will replace ISDN for high-volume Internet users, and the monthly fee will fall as competition increases. An installation fee of up to £150 is also payable.

At present roughly 35% of UK telephone customers could have ADSL service, and this will increase to 70% by 2002. It depends on the speed with which BT converts its telephone exchanges. Customers must also live within three miles of their local exchange.

Freeserve (*www.freeserve.co.uk*) and Claranet (*www.clara.net*) offer ADSL services too, but they also depend on BT having equipped your local exchange for you to be able to use them.

One problem with ADSL is that if your computer is on-line permanently it will be vulnerable to attack from other Internet users. To prevent this it is recommended that you switch off the computer when you are not using it and also install **firewall** software which will stop unauthorised access to your computer. Your ADSL supplier should be able to recommend suitable firewall software.

TIME TO GET CONNECTED!

You should receive instructions with your new computer or CD-ROM disk. The steps involved are:

- Make sure your modem is connected correctly or installed inside the computer.

- Insert the disk in the CD-ROM drive. It should start automatically.

- An installation program, called a **Wizard**, will ask for information. Answer the questions carefully.

- You will be asked for an account name to use with the ISP's service. Choose something that others will recognise, maybe based on your name. You might have to combine names or numbers to find one that has not been registered with the ISP already. Account names must be unique with each service provider, so there can only be one 'johnsmith'. If you choose a name that has already been taken, the ISP will suggest others, which you can either accept or reject.

- You will also be asked for a password, which must be known only to you. It must be something that others will not be able to guess so don't use your name, address, phone number or postcode. Some ISPs demand a mixture of letters and numbers. You will have to enter it twice, to make sure that you spelled it correctly. Keep it private.

Once you have set up the account, make sure that you write down your account name for future reference. Remember your password. Do not write it down with your account name.

Each time you **log in** to your ISP you will have to enter your account name and password. The on-screen dial-up connection box will have your account name in it with a space for your password to be entered. You can automate this by ticking the checkbox marked 'Save password'. Only use this facility if your computer is kept somewhere private, otherwise others could log in without your permission.

Problems?
Your ISP will have a help-desk for you to phone in times of trouble. The charges for phoning them vary from free to 50 pence

Fig. 2. Enter your name and password when logging in. The password
is replaced by stars to prevent others from seeing it.

per minute. They are usually quite good at sorting out your
problems. Have a pen and paper ready to write down what they
say. You cannot speak to them and log in at the same time, unless
you have two phone lines.

If they are not very helpful, go to another ISP. There are plenty
of them to choose from.

2

Getting in Touch with Others

Writing is a solitary occupation, but contact with others is always valuable and the Internet can make communication with like-minded people anywhere in the world both simple and inexpensive. There are four ways of communicating with others:

- electronic mail
- newsgroups
- chat lines or chat rooms
- desktop conferencing and Internet telephony.

ELECTRONIC MAIL (OR EMAIL)

One of the greatest benefits of the Internet has to be electronic mail, or **email**. It is the most-used Internet service. The major benefits are:

- instant transmission of messages
- no postal charges
- ability to send files such as word-processed documents, pictures and programs
- opportunity to send copies of messages to as many people as you wish all at once
- the message gets to the recipient/s even if they are not at their desks, e.g. asleep in Australia (or England).

The real beauty of email is that the recipient may read and consider the message when it is convenient. Unlike telephone conversations, there is no pressure for instant replies, so you can give messages your full attention and respond when both the time and your reply are right, and unlike **snail mail**, the email users' name for the postal system, there is no delay while waiting for the post to be delivered.

Many publishers are now accepting submissions by email. The text can be received and put straight into the computer used to produce the book or magazine. An article may be transmitted in a few seconds. A 50,000-word book can go in a couple of minutes. However, it is vital to check that the publisher is willing to accept your submissions in this form. Reading unsolicited manuscripts on-screen can be tedious.

Simple email

Email works by the sender typing messages into an email program and storing them in the computer until they are all ready to be sent. The sender then logs on to the service provider and sends all the messages at once. The messages go to the recipients' service providers, where they will be stored on computers awaiting collection.

When the recipients log on to the Internet they **download** (or collect) the waiting messages. Once the messages have been received, the telephone line can be disconnected and the messages read **off-line**, so saving telephone costs.

Sending messages

To send messages you need to use an email program, such as **Microsoft Outlook Express** or **Netscape Navigator**. These programs allow you to construct a message and, once it is finished, store it in a mail folder called **Outbox** or **Unsent messages**. When all your messages are ready, connect to the service provider and dispatch them.

Where do I send the message to?
Before you can send a message you will need the email address of your correspondent. The simplest way to find it is to ask. A quick phone call can save a lot of time searching. Your email program has an **address book** in which you can store names, email addresses, phone numbers, postal addresses and other details for your contacts.

What does the email address mean?
A typical address looks like:

myname@myisp.com

where 'myname' is the name of the recipient and 'myisp.com' is the name of the internet service provider.

Where do I get my email address from?
Your email address will be set up when you first start your account with an ISP. You will be asked to provide an email name and it will be accepted if it has not been chosen by someone else before you. Most ISPs will allow you a number of addresses, so you can have one or more for personal use and others for each aspect of your writing life (readers' responses to articles, messages from editors and so on). Family members can also have their own addresses.

Where do I find people's email addresses?

As mentioned above, the easiest way is simply to exchange addresses. However, if you do not have the information, there are other ways of finding them.

Searching for email addresses
Many **search engines** (computers you can use to find information) now provide email address search facilities. You go to the email search area on the search engine's Web site and enter the details asked for, usually the person's surname, forename and (maybe) the address or service provider (if known). There are so many email users, many of whose accounts are rarely or never used, that it can be difficult.

See the appendix for a list of sites that find email addresses.

But how do I actually send a message?

Simple!

- Start your email program.

- Click on the 'New message' button and fill in the box provided.

- Type the recipient's email address in the 'To:' box.

- Put a title in the 'Subject' box.

- Type the message in the main area below the subject.

- When you are happy with it, click on the 'Send' button.

If you are **on-line**, that is, connected to your Internet service, you can send your message immediately. If not, it will be stored in the 'Outbox' or 'Unsent mail' folder until you are next on-line. The most efficient way of working is to edit all your messages and save them in your 'Outbox', then send them all at once when you connect to your service provider. You can do this by clicking on the 'Send/Receive' button. All your messages will be sent and any new messages waiting for you will be received.

Here is a message being edited using Outlook Express:

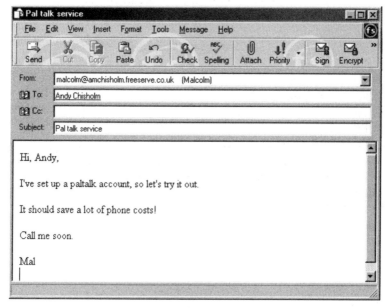

Fig. 3.

If the recipient's address is taken from the address book, as above, only the name is shown.

Receiving messages

Messages will be received when your email program is running and you are logged on to your ISP. Once you have sent and received your messages, go off-line and browse through the newly-arrived mail. You may print messages if you wish.

Your email program will allow you to set up folders (like filing cabinet drawers) to store your messages. You can set up as many folders as you want, perhaps one for each correspondent or for each different publisher you write for.

Fig. 4. Outlook Express screen showing my folders (left window), list of messages in the highlighted folder, my Inbox (upper right window) and the contents of the highlighted message (lower right)

Email text limitations

There is one limitation to email. The text is usually sent in a form called **ASCII**, or **plain text**. It cannot be formatted into bold, italic, etc. This may be a problem when you want to emphasize your text. To overcome this problem, you should use a word processor to write your book or article and send it as a **file attachment** which is linked to your message. You will also find that some editors want **hard copy** (i.e. a printed manuscript) which you will have to send by post.

Attaching a file to a message

Your word-processed article can be attached to your message very simply. While you are composing the message:

• Click on the 'Attach' or 'Attachment' button.

- Supply the name of the file, including its directory/ies.

- Click on 'Attach' in the dialogue box.

When you send the message, it will show the name of the attached file and the recipient will be offered the chance to see it immediately or to save it until later. You can attach word-processed documents, databases, spreadsheets, pictures, music – in fact anything which can be saved as a computer file.

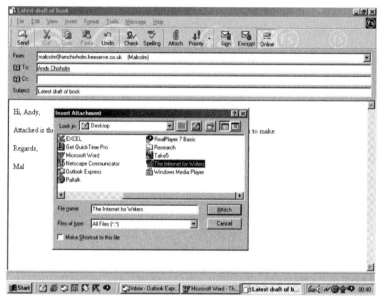

Fig. 5.   See how the dialogue box appears to allow you to search for files you want to attach to the message. Click on 'Attach' and the file will be sent with the message.

NEWSGROUPS

Newsgroups are similar to email, but messages are **posted** to a publicly-viewable, electronic notice board. Anyone can post messages and anyone else may read them. To use newsgroups you need a **newsreader** program. Internet Explorer and Netscape Messenger both include newsreaders. There are over 30,000 newsgroups and they cover almost every subject imaginable, writing included.

To use them you must first download the newsgroup list from

your ISP. This will take a few minutes, but you are collecting a lot of data. Once the list has been received you can go off-line while you select which groups to subscribe to. Don't be worried about the cost of subscribing; it is all free.

How do I subscribe to newsgroups?

Once you have downloaded the list of newsgroups you can select a few to look at. Start by choosing one or two, just to see how it works. In the newsgroup subscriptions dialogue box, type the subject word you want to look for, such as 'writing' or 'poetry'. The program will then display all the newsgroups with your word in their titles. Beware! 'Writing' covers many aspects of writing as the frame below shows. Notice that creative writing, journalism, Dr Who and graffiti all appear!

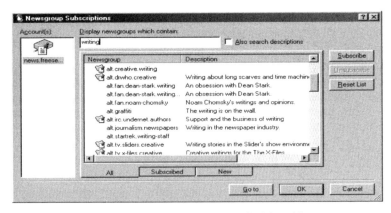

Fig. 6. Newsgroups all connected with writing.

When you find something that looks interesting, click on it and then click on 'Subscribe'. A symbol will appear by the name of the newsgroup to show that you have subscribed to it.

When you have finished setting up your subscriptions, you have to decide whether to receive just the **headers** (or titles) of the messages or to receive them complete. If you subscribe to a large, busy newsgroup then downloading all the messages could take a long time. If you just receive the headers at first, you can select which ones to read and download them later.

The advantage of newsgroups is that when comments are posted they are grouped with the original item (this is called a

thread), so making it easy to follow related items. Beware, though, of the fact that anyone can post information and claim to be a *bona fide* writer or informed critic.

Which newsgroups are best for me as a writer?

This will take some working out. The easiest way to find out is to try them. Download the current postings (the newsgroup word for messages) and see if they interest you. Most writing newsgroups are a mixture of news and requests for help or criticism. Here is a list of some for you to try:

Journalism:
Alt.journalism.freelance

Fiction:
Post your fiction here for comment, read the work of others and share news . . .

Alt.creative.writing	news, comment, and fiction posted
Alt.fiction.original	original fiction
Alt.horror.creative	original horror fiction

Poetry:
Read poetry, comment on it, post your own work and share news here . . .
Alt.arts.poetry
Rec.arts.poems

Related to particular authors:
For comments and news about particular authors . . .
Alt.books.*authorname*
Alt.fan.*authorname*
e.g. alt.books.arthur-clarke, alt.fan.douglas-adams, alt.fan.authors.stephen-king

Web site design and writing
Comp.infosystems.www.authoring.html
Uk.net.web.authoring

Searching for newsgroups

The search engine **deja news** (*www.deja.com*) is devoted to newsgroups and allows a more sophisticated means of finding news groups than by simply entering words into the newsgroup subscriptions box in your newsreader program. Its content has recently been taken over by Google and now looks like the Google search engine, but it still searches newgroups. Google is gradually adding new features to the service. Find the revamped version at *http://groups.google.com/.*

CHAT ROOMS

Chat rooms are web sites where participants may chat using their keyboards. Access is gained by going to the page and clicking on the appropriate room. Freeserve has chat rooms based on ages (teens, twentysomethings, sixtyplus, etc.) and by subject (arts and culture, music, etc.) at *www.freeserve.com/chat.* Most search engines also have chat facilities. Try out Yahoo! (*www.yahoo.com*) or check your own ISP's home page to see if they have a chat facility.

When you enter a room you are asked for a name to be known by for the duration of your presence. It is a good idea to use a pseudonym. Most Internet chat users do. You will see people's names and comments on screen and you add your comments as you think fit. It is a good idea to watch the chat flow for a little while to see if it is of interest. There are often a number of threads to the chat in a room. Each comment is preceded by the speaker's name so that you can see who to reply to.

Beware!

Chat room users are totally anonymous. You have no way of knowing who they really are. Because of this they can be quite unruly in their manner. Be polite, accept what others say (it is their opinion, after all) and put your own point firmly. If you do not like the way a conversation is going, you can always leave.

Never exchange addresses or phone numbers until you are absolutely sure who it is that you are dealing with. Some would say that it is inadvisable even to give your email address. If you arrange to meet someone as a result of a chat room encounter, make sure that it is in a public place. Take a trusted friend with you at first. Remember that people often change their ages, genders and other personal details when chatting and emailing to strangers. They can be a funny lot!

Start your own chat room
Once you are familiar with chat rooms, why not arrange for
yourself and your friends to have your own chat room? A number
of ISPs now allow you to have private chat facilities. You can start
your own on-line writers' circle. The big advantage is that you can
set aside a fixed time to meet, every day, week or however
frequently you want.

You can limit the membership to people you want to join. It can
reflect the operation of the Writers' Folio or Poetry Folio, in
which work is placed in a folder and passed from one writer to the
next, round-robin-style, for criticism. In the past this has been
done using the postal system, which can take a long time if
the group is large as only one person holds the folder at any one
time.

In the private chat room, you can submit work for comment and
have a number of responses as soon as they are ready. Members
may print the work or save the screen for off-line consideration
and go back on-line to post comments and read the criticism from
others. The only problem with this system is that it is designed for
instant chat in short sentences. Long pieces might fill a screen
before you could print the work for consideration.

It might be better to use a mail list, which uses email messaging
for the same purpose. Members can peruse work off-line and
comment at their leisure. See Chapter 5, On-line Help, for more
information.

DESK-TOP CONFERENCING

One of the most efficient facilities on the Internet is **desk-top
conferencing**. This means using the Internet to connect between
two or more computers to exchange information on-line. Conferencing happens in **real time**. It is private, accessible only to the
computers that have joined it. Outsiders cannot participate except
when invited. Unlike chat rooms, there is no central computer
hosting the event.

All participants are on-line at the same time. They can:

- exchange text messages

- exchange files (e.g. word-processed documents, databases or
  spreadsheets)

- jointly manipulate **applications** (e.g. joint word processing or image editing) where both participants can modify the screen at the same time

- speak to each other (e.g. to discuss or criticise manuscripts)

- see each other or show each other objects with cameras

- combine any of the above.

There are various programs available for conferencing. *Paltalk* (email: *support@paltalk.com*) enables users to nominate 'on-line pals'. When you log in, it immediately tells you whether your 'pals' are on- or off-line. If they are not on-line, make a quick phone call to ask them to go on-line and then log back onto Paltalk for local rate conversations around the world. It is possible to have multi-way conferences, which add enormous value to conferencing. Another widely used service is *ICQ*, an abbreviation for 'I seek you' (*www.icq.com*). To use these services all participants must be registered with the same organisation.

The disadvantage is that the digitising and transmission process takes time, so you have to be a little patient, allowing half a second or so for your voice to reach your partner and for the other voice to return. You also have to hold down a key on the keyboard when you speak. Video images need to send a lot of data and the available bandwidth through a modem is limited, so pictures tend to be jerky. However, with a little practice you can get a lot of value out of Internet conferencing.

Conferencing services allow you to look for 'instant' contacts, so that you can start communicating straight away. Some offer the opportunity to register your interests, enabling others with similar interests to contact you.

3

Surfing the Web

THE WORLD WIDE WEB

The World Wide Web (or the Web or just WWW) is the best-known face of the Internet. **Web pages** are bright, colourful pages of text, images, sound and animations. The Web has grown in popularity because it is very easy to use.

The advent of fierce competition between Internet Service Providers (ISPs) has led them to give Web space to anyone who wants it at little or no cost, so people can display (or post) whatever information they like. There is little or no control over what can be found:

- University professors and researchers post learned articles.

- Teenagers of the sixties and seventies post information on the Beatles and the Rolling Stones while current teens post details of today's idols.

- Anarchists describe how to make bombs and create disorder.

- Animal lovers show off pictures of their pets.

- Businesses use it as a shop window for selling anything and everything, from groceries to pornography.

WHAT IS THE WORLD WIDE WEB?

The Web is a network of computers which display information in the form of pages of coloured text and images. They can also carry sound and moving pictures. Pages are linked to enable easy access from one to another by means of **hot links**. Users do not need to know where in the world the pages come from. They are passed automatically across the Web from the **host** (or supplier) to the recipient.

The Web is so enormous that computers called **search engines** are used to locate information on your chosen subject. Just type the subject that you want to look up into a search page and a few seconds later you will be given an index of links to pages of related information.

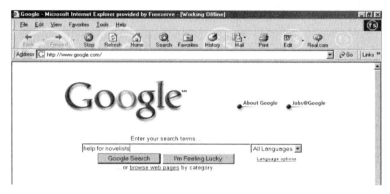

Fig. 7. Typing a search query into the Google search engine.

What are web pages and how do I read them?

Web pages are ordinary text with special effects commands embedded into them.

These commands are written in **Hypertext Markup Language (HTML)**. The **Web Browser** program interprets the HTML commands to produce the page formatting, hot links and graphical effects on the computer screen.

Any computer may be used to view Web pages as long as a Web browser program has been written for it. Web browsers all do the same job, but they are written for specific computers. Some digital television set-top boxes also have them built in to enable you to view Web pages on your TV. **WAP** mobile telephones now have Web browsers incorporated into them.

The best way to choose a Web browser is to try several out. Your selection is a matter of personal preference from those available for your computer.

Take your pick of the browsers

The browser you choose must run on your computer. There has been a lot of competition between **Microsoft Internet Explorer** and **Netscape Navigator** for domination of the Apple and IBM PC-compatible markets, so you will find that you are inundated with CD-ROMs containing them. Most Internet-related magazines have cover disks that include one or the other. There are browsers available for other makes of computer but you may have to pay for them. If you have a smaller PC, you may find that the Opera Web browser runs better.

There is a browser page on the Yahoo site at *http://dir.yahoo.com/computers_and_internet/software/internet/ world_wide_web/browsers/* where you can find links to information about many browsers, including comparisons and new developments.

FINDING INFORMATION

There are three ways to locate Web information:

- You know the address (or **URL**) of the page and type it in.

- You click on a **hot link** from a known page.

- You use a **search engine**.

You know the page address

If you know the page address, called the **Uniform Resource Locator (URL)**, then type it in to the 'Address' or 'Location' box near the top of the browser page and press the <Enter> key. The browser will send the address into the Internet and a few seconds later the page will appear. It does not matter whether the page comes from down the road or from the other side of the world. It will still arrive in exactly the same way and (usually) within a few seconds.

Hint: go straight into the address box
Press the <Tab> key to move straight into the 'Address' or 'Location' box. There is no need to use the mouse or to delete the current entry, just type the URL, leaving out the 'http://' part (the browser will assume that it is there and will display it when the page arrives).

Fig. 8.

What does the URL tell me?
The URL gives an indication of where the page is located on the Web. There are up to five parts:

1. 'http://' All Web page URLs start with this. It stands for **hypertext transfer protocol** and it tells the computer that you are using a Web page.
2. **Domain name** (name of the Web site). It may include '**www**'.
3. Type of organisation, e.g. **co** or **com** (commercial), **org** (non-commercial organisation) or **net** (Internet-related organisation), but these are not used in some countries.
4. Country code (not used if American or international).
5. Path to a file or sub-directory within the domain.

Here is an example:

http://www.writers.org.uk/society

http://	tells us that it is a Web page.
www	also tells us that it is a Web page, but it is not always used.
writers	is the name of the domain.
org	says that it is a non-commercial organisation.
uk	tells us that it is in the United Kingdom.
/society	is a sub-directory or area within the 'writers' domain.

(The 'writers' domain is a joint venture between the Authors' Licensing and Collecting Society, The Society of Authors and The Writers' Guild of Great Britain.)

Using a hot link
If you see some coloured, underlined text (a **hot link**) on the page, then you may click on it to jump to another, related page. As you point to this hot link you will see a reference to the linked page on the **status bar** at the bottom of the browser screen. You will also see the pointer (or cursor) change to a hand with a pointing index finger. This confirms that your pointer is over a hot link.

Images can also be used as hot links. As with text links, the pointer will change to a pointing hand. These are sometimes used in interactive maps to zoom in to see larger scale plans of an area or to find information about a location. A photograph may lead to information about a personality. A small picture (or 'thumbnail' image) may reveal a larger, more detailed, view. Click on the picture and see the details.

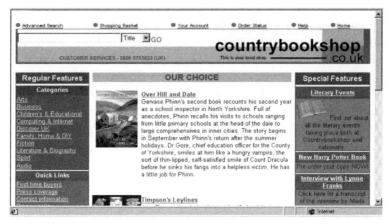

Fig. 9.   The underlined words and the images all act as hot links at the Country Book Shop's home page.

Using a search engine

A search engine is a Web site that can help you find information about almost anything. It uses a large, powerful computer to keep records of the contents of thousands of millions of Web pages. Using one can be very simple indeed, especially when you consider how much information it can give you. There are two ways to use a search engine:

- You enter the subject you are looking for and tell it to search.

- You click on **topic links or headings** to find what you want.

You have to know the address of the search engine you want to use. You will decide which ones you prefer as you gain experience. These are a few popular engines:

Alta Vista	*www.altavista.com*
Excite	*www.excite.com*
Google	*www.google.com*
Infoseek UK	*www.infoseek.co.uk*
Lycos	*www.lycos.co.uk*

Yahoo UK   *www.yahoo.co.uk*
37.com   *www.37.com* (checks up to 37 search engines for
               your query!)

Searching for your subject

Once you have the search engine page on your screen, click in the
'Search' dialogue box, type in a word or phrase you want to look
for and click on the 'Find', 'Search' or 'Go' button on the screen.
Some will also let you press the <Enter> key to start the search.

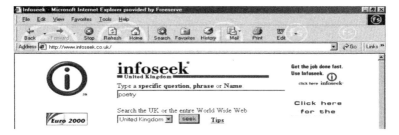

Fig. 10.   Searching for information about poetry using Infoseek UK.

The search engine will spend a few seconds searching its
records to find which pages contain the words you have entered.
It will then list the most accurate matches on an **index page**. This
page contains references to (typically) 10 to 20 Web pages. For
each page listed there will be:

- a brief description

- a percentage estimate of the accuracy or relevance of the
  match

- the URL

- a hot link to take you directly to the page.

Click on the hot link and you're there.

Hint:
With Internet Explorer hold down <Shift> as you click on the hot
link and a new window will open, leaving the search page still

accessible in the background. If you use this you do not have to wait to go back to the search page. You can also have several pages opened at once and switch between them.

Fig. 11.   Infoseek UK has found 311,321 pages relating to poetry.

If the page is not what you are looking for, click on the browser's 'Back' button (near the top left corner of the screen) to return to the index page and choose another link. If you exhaust the offered pages, look at the bottom of the index page and you will find that you can go to further (or 'next') index pages with more offerings from the search engine.

If you search for one word, such as 'writing' or 'poetry', the search engine may tell you that it has found hundreds, thousands or maybe even millions of pages. The next chapter will tell you how to improve your searching techniques so that you get the results you want quickly and efficiently.

Topic links
Some search engines also have hot links to many subject areas which users are frequently looking for, such as:

Fig. 11.   Lycos (*www.lycos.co.uk*) topic index. Click on a link to expand the topic.

- arts
- cars
- entertainment
- health
- news and current affairs
- road maps
- shopping
- travel
- women's concerns.

Pointing at these 'topic links' will take you to further menus which help to refine your search. This is done solely by clicking on hot links.

HOW FAST DOES THE INFORMATION ARRIVE?

The speed of arrival of information depends on five factors:

- the page content
- how busy the host site is
- the speed of the slowest link in the chain from the site host computer to yours
- how many other people are using the Internet
- the speed of your modem (the faster the modem, the sooner the page arrives).

Page content

Pages can consist of pure text or they may include graphical images. Text arrives very quickly. A complete screen full of text uses a maximum of only 2000 bytes (or characters) of data. This will take only a second or so to arrive. A picture may use many thousands or millions of bytes of data and so may take many seconds to arrive. There are various techniques used to reduce this delay but complex graphics may still increase the download time to tens of seconds. This can be very frustrating when you are waiting and, perhaps, paying for the time.

The host site

The site that holds the page you want to view deals with requests on a first-come-first-served basis. If lots of pages are being requested you may have to wait a few seconds for yours to be despatched. Some host computers are not really fast enough to cope with the demands placed upon them, which will further slow down the responses.

Modem speed

As mentioned in Chapter 1, various technologies exist to connect your computer to your ISP. The absolute minimum speed of modem you should use can receive data at 28,800 bits per second (bps or baud) which is equivalent to 2,880 characters per second. Most modern modems work at up to 56,000 bps. The faster modems can download data at up to twice the speed of the slower. So make sure that you have the fastest modem you can afford. If you are served by a cable television company, you may be able to use a cable modem which goes even faster than 56,000 bps.

British Telecom provides a service called **Home Highway**. This is a high speed **ISDN** (Integrated Services Digital Network) service which provides two 64,000 bps channels. They may be combined to give 128,000 bps or allow you to work at 64,000 bps and use the second channel to make phone calls while you are surfing. If you do a lot of Internet work, this relatively expensive service may well be worthwhile.

Even faster than ISDN is a new service, called **ADSL** (Asymmetric Digital Subscriber Line). It was launched in September 2000. BT's ADSL service is called **BT Openworld**. It is an internet service provider and a very fast cable connection, supplying email addresses, Web space and additional content for subscribers. It costs a fixed charge of £40 per month, but it does deliver data at a speed of at least 512 Kbps and up to 2 Mbps (two million bits per second), i.e. up to 40 times the speed of the best current modems. The big advantages of ADSL over ordinary telephone access are:

- the monthly cost is fixed (no Internet telephone call charges)
- includes the cost of an ADSL modem

- very fast data delivery

- you can use the telephone at the same time as you use the Internet.

Availability of ADSL and BT Openworld is gradually spreading round the country. Whether or not you can have the service depends on various factors, so contact BT on *www.bt.com/adsl* if you want to find out more.

Other ISPs will also offer ADSL when the local telephone cable from the exchange to your home (called the 'local loop') is opened up to competition in 2001.

The slowest link

Your data arrives from the host computer by way of a series of links from one computer to another. The speed of each link is dependent on the computers at each end and the traffic they are carrying. If one link is carrying a lot of traffic, it slows down the rate at which your data will arrive. Traffic levels increase enormously when America wakes up, so do any large quantities of downloading in the mornings.

It is at evenings and weekends that most people spend time surfing, so your ISP may suffer from increased response times, again slowing down the rate of arrival of your data.

Also check the 'Speed and Availability' listings in *Internet* magazine. Your ISP may provide a fast service which is masked by slow links from the site you are visiting or it may be the other way round, a slow ISP masking a fast site.

Speeding it up – turn off images

Images can increase the time taken to download pages considerably. If you know that you will be receiving lots of images and that you do not need to look at them, you can turn them off. Then you will only receive the text, which takes far less time to arrive.

To turn off the loading of images with Internet Explorer:

1. On the 'Tools' menu in Internet Explorer, click 'Internet Options'.
2. Click the 'Advanced' tab.
3. In the 'Multimedia' area (it is quite a long way down the list), remove the ticks from one or more of the 'Show pictures',

'Play animations', 'Play videos', or 'Play sounds' check boxes by clicking on them.

If the 'Show pictures' or 'Play videos' check box is cleared, you can still display an individual picture or animation on a Web page by right clicking its icon and then clicking 'Show Picture'.

To turn off the loading of images with Netscape Navigator:

1. From the 'Edit' menu, choose 'Preferences'.
2. Click 'Advanced' in the category column.
3. Remove the tick from the check box labelled 'Automatically load images' by clicking on it.

Hint: saving the page for later
Once you have received a page, save it to read or print later, when you are off line. To save a page:
    On the 'File' menu, click 'Save as'
    Use the dialogue box to save it in your preferred folder. You may change the name if you wish.

BOOKMARKING PAGES

When you find a page that you use regularly (e.g. the train timetables or Webster's Dictionary) or that you may want to return to at some future time, it is a good idea to **bookmark** it. Your browser software will have a 'Favorites' (Internet Explorer) or 'Bookmark' (Netscape Navigator) facility that allows you to store the page reference in a file. Then, when you next go surfing, you will be able to return to your preferred page(s) simply by clicking on the name of that page.

To add the page you are viewing to the bookmark list:

• Click on 'Favorites' or 'Bookmark'.

• Click on 'Add page'.

When you next want to go to the page:

• Click on 'Favorites' or 'Bookmark'.

• Click on the page reference in the list.

Both Internet Explorer and Netscape Navigator allow you to have your most-used bookmarks on screen at all times. Explorer lists them down the side of the screen when you click on the 'Favorites' button, while Netscape places them across the screen on the Personal **Toolbar** just below the Location box. Explorer also has a Links toolbar, which may be customised to display links to regularly visited Web pages, just below the Address toolbar. You might find this a useful facility, or you may regard it as a waste of screen space, reducing the size of the page you can see in your browser.

REMEMBERING WHERE YOU HAVE BEEN

Browsers remember the addresses of sites you have visited recently. You can set how far back they remember:

Using Internet Explorer	Using Netscape Navigator
• Click on 'Tools' menu.	• Click on 'Edit' menu.
• Select 'Internet options'.	• Select 'Preferences'.
• Enter the number of days to be remembered.	• Enter the number of days to be remembered in the history box.
• Click 'OK'.	• Click 'OK'.

Every page you visit will be remembered for the time you set as shown above. Once the time limit is reached the page reference is discarded.

To revisit a page in the history list press <CTRL><H> (i.e. hold down the key marked 'Ctrl' and press the 'H' key). This applies to both Explorer and Navigator.

Hint: use a search engine as your home page
All browsers store the URL of one page that is designated the **home page**. This is the page you reach when you click on the browser's 'home page' button. When you are researching, make it the URL of your preferred search engine so that you can get to it immediately.

How to set the home page:

Using Internet Explorer:	Using Netscape Navigator:
• Click on the 'Tools' menu.	• Click on the 'Edit' menu.
• Click on 'Internet options'.	• Click on 'Preferences'.
• Select the 'General' tab.	• Under 'Home page' enter the home page URL.
• Under 'Home page' enter the home page URL.	• Click on 'OK'.
• Click on 'OK'.	

Do you want to start up at the last page you visited?

When you are involved in continuing research, you may wish to return to the last page you visited during your previous Web browsing session. To set this option using Netscape Navigator:

• Click on 'Edit' menu.

• Click on 'Preferences'.

• Under 'Navigator starts with' point and click on 'Last page visited'.

4

Advanced Searching Techniques

Putting one word into a search engine will find you information, but it will often find far too much, such as the 311,321 references to poetry found in Chapter 3. There are a number of ways to narrow down the search. Using the techniques shown here will help you to get straight to the information you need.

HOW IS THE WEB ORGANISED?

In short, it isn't. At least, there is no formal indexing. Anyone and everyone (including you) can set up a page or a site and display anything at all. The only way to find information is by using a **search engine**.

HOW DOES A SEARCH ENGINE WORK?

Search engines store details of millions of Web sites and pages. They collect information by looking round the Internet and seeing what appears on pages that they find. Web site operators register their sites and pages by subject in order to make sure that their details are available. Without this, Web pages could not be found and a great deal of information would be almost impossible to locate. It would be like trying to find your way round a strange city without the aid of a map or people to give you directions.

HOW DO I SEARCH EFFECTIVELY?

First, note that no two search engines work in exactly the same way, so you will find that not all these instructions will work every time. However, they will give you a good start.

Single word searches

As you saw in Chapter 3, you can enter a single word into a search engine and you will receive many, many results. This may be useful for general knowledge reading about a subject, but you will not do much specialist searching like this. Type the word into the search box, click on the 'Go', 'Search' or 'Find' button and wait for the results.

Using word combinations

It is far more effective to combine words in order to limit the number of pages found and to improve the likelihood of these pages containing what you want to know. The main techniques for narrowing down searches are:

- using phrases

- capitalising names

- using + and - in front of words

- using 'wildcards'.

Using phrases

If you are writing an article about King Arthur and his round table, you might want to look for Web pages with the words 'round' and 'table'. A search engine would (usually) look for all pages containing the word 'round' and all those containing 'table'. They would be listed starting with the pages which contained both words, but not necessarily together. To find the phrase as a whole, enter it into the engine surrounded by double quote marks:

"round table"

Capitalising names

When searching for names of people or organisations, such as the Round Table, use capital first letters:

Round Table

Using + and - signs

To ensure that a word is included in a Web page, put a plus sign (+) immediately in front of it.

If you do not want pages which refer to a particular word, precede it with a minus (-). So to find pages about grammar, but not about grammar schools, use the search:

+grammar -school

Some search engines, such as Google (*www.google.com*) automatically include all words in the search term. This is more convenient than having to remember to use the + prefix, but you still need to use the - prefix to avoid words that you do not want.

*Wildcards ***

Wildcards are used to expand a search. An asterisk or a question mark (depending on the search engine) is placed in a word or phrase and the search engine will substitute different characters in its place:

'comp*' would expand to competition, compose, computer, etc.
'writ*' would expand to writer, writing, written, etc.

Not all search engines have this facility.

Fig. 13.   A search for +"golf club"+Southport-Formby found 897 matching web pages which included Southport golf clubs but none in Formby.

Search engines have comprehensive help pages. This is important, because although most of them have similar ways of interpreting search terms, they all have minor differences. A few minutes spent downloading and reading the help pages will be a good investment as you should be able to improve your searching techniques enormously, thus saving time and improving accuracy.

How you can alter search terms to narrow down the results
Using phrases in double quotation marks is a good way to improve searches. Look at the results below of using different phrases when searching for on-line writers' groups. While using the Google search engine:

- **on-line writers circle** produced over 38,000 results

- **on-line writers circles** produced over 19,000 results

- "**on-line writers**" produced 497 results

- "**on-line writers group**" produced 24 results

- "**on-line writers circle**" produced only one.

5

On-line Help

A big problem for many writers is preparing the text in the correct style and format. Publishers may be deterred from accepting an article or story if it is grammatically incorrect, or if the style is poor or wrong for the publication. The Internet has hundreds of sites devoted to helping writers with just these problems. They can be divided into two types:

- those which give active help from other writers
- reference sites.

UNIVERSITIES

Many writing sites are linked to universities and colleges that run courses in creative writing. There are pages devoted to grammar, style and presentation. It is important to remember that several of them are American and so use American spelling, grammar and vocabulary.

One excellent site is the Trace on-line writing community. This is hosted by Nottingham Trent University at *http://trace.ntu.ac.uk*. Contact them by email at *trace@ntu.ac.uk*. This site has pages of general help for writers, with useful links to other sites, but it also runs **conferences** on dozens of topics of interest to writers. They include poetry, prose, scriptwriting, feminism, children's writing, workshops, opinion and a technical forum. Some are on-going, while others run their natural course and are then left on-line as a reference. Contributions come from all round the world.

BUBL, a service aimed at higher education, has links to writing resources. Go to *http://bubl.ac.uk/link/w/* and follow the writing links. They offer many further links to sites that deal with writing, including writing laboratories, help services and email-distributed newsletters. It is part of the BUBL site, whose BUBL Link page (*www.bubl.ac.uk/link/*) offers access to Internet resources on all academic subject areas.

Another useful link is *www.kelly.mcmail.com*. This site has articles, hints and tips on how to write situation comedies for film, theatre, radio and TV. It has links with Birkbeck College, part of the University of London, which runs commercial courses for writers.

OWLs (ON-LINE WRITING LABORATORIES)

A number of universities and other organisations have set up **OWLs**. These sites give help on a wide range of writing subjects, with special emphasis on grammar, spelling and presentation.

OWLs are run by universities and colleges chiefly for the benefit of their students, both on campus and distance learners. They deal with all aspects of creative, technical, business and social writing. The World Wide Web is the preferred medium for administering OWLs because of its universality. Teaching materials and information can be very easily distributed and at very little cost compared with the number of students who can access them.

You will find everything for the developing writer:

- lesson notes on all aspects of writing
- lecture presentations
- on-line courses
- links to reference sources
- help with style
- help with grammar
- access to scholarly web sites
- literary web sites
- search engines
- research methods
- newsletters
- links to other OWLs.

Most OWLs are run by American universities, so you have to watch the spelling (it is all in American English) but it can be

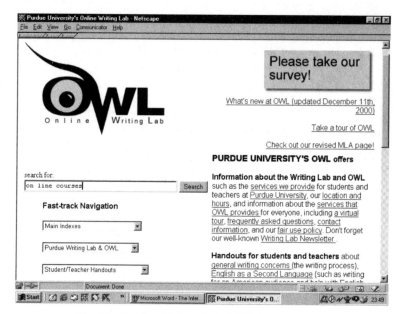

Fig. 14. Purdue University's OWL home page at
http://owl.english.purdue.edu.

especially helpful if you are trying to sell to the United States.
You must remember that OWLs are provided for the use of the
universities' students, and that outsiders are guests. Make sure
that you read the 'terms of use' information and abide by it. If the
services are abused we may find that they disappear from public
view.

LOCAL WRITERS' CIRCLES

Many writers' circles have their own Web sites, usually to
advertise their presence in the community. They want to attract
new members living locally. Others run on-line sessions, offering
advice on a mutual self-help basis. Look at *www.author.co.uk* for
a list of UK circles. At the time of writing, a downloadable list is
promised but has not yet appeared.

ON-LINE WRITERS' CIRCLES

Writers' circles have a long tradition of helping writers to develop
their work. The on-line circle is a natural development of the

regular meeting, but, of course, membership is no longer restricted to where you live. Anyone in the world can join and make use of the facilities.

Email-based writers' groups (mailing lists)

Mailing lists are email-based groups. They are probably the most efficient to use. Writers send items for discussion or criticism to an email address. From there they are sent by email to all the group members, who can either reply to the group address (from where the replies are sent out to all members) or they can reply to the original writer direct. This has the advantage of allowing both public discussion of a piece and the opportunity for individuals to give direct responses.

Some discussion groups are moderated. This means that the group operator will read all messages as they arrive to ensure that they are relevant and will not offend group members. (It is an unfortunate fact of life that the Internet, being anonymous, can bring out the worst in people.)

Because membership of an email-based group can be limited, unsuitable subscribers can be removed. This helps to ensure that criticism will be from those who are in the right position to give it. The mailing list is often a very friendly place as membership numbers tend to be relatively small. Contributors are usually generous with their constructive criticism.

When you join a group, look at the messages to see what sort of things are discussed. When you have the 'feel' of the group, then try introducing yourself and asking a question. It is a facet of email etiquette to be polite and try to help others if you can, but do make sure that any information you give out is accurate. Similarly, make sure that you verify any information you receive. Well-meaning people do sometimes get things wrong. Also, make sure that your topics for discussion are acceptable to the group. If it specialises in gothic novel writing, don't start asking about writing science fiction – you will soon discover that you are not wanted.

If there is no group discussing your areas of interest, start your own group at Yahoo! groups (*www.groups.yahoo.com*).

Where do I find these mailing list groups?
The easiest way to look for mailing lists is to type the words 'mail list' or 'mailto' into a search engine. Google (*www.google.com*) returned over 50,000 references. One good site which is intended

as a one-stop information resource about email discussion groups or 'lists', as they are sometimes called, is at *www.webcom.com/impulse/list.html.*

The webcom site (*www.webcom.com*) has information on mail list services, how to find out which lists are available, what they cover, and how to join them. It also has details of software for running your own mail lists, mail list commands for subscribing and unsubscribing, and pages of frequently asked questions (FAQs).

The Yahoo! groups site (*www.groups.yahoo.com*) points to a great many writing mail lists. Over 90 categories include screenwriting, science fiction, novels, short stories, magazine writing and technical writing, and over 2000 groups are included. To use the service you will need to register with Yahoo!, supplying them with an ID name and password.

Newsgroup-based circles

Newsgroups and how to join them are mentioned in Chapter 2. They are worth a mention here simply to say that they are a useful forum where writers can get together in order to show off their work and receive comments. However, they are totally public. Anyone may read them and post comments. Sometimes they are moderated, but this can be difficult if there are very many contributors.

REFERENCE SITES

Have you ever thought just how useful it would be to have all the world's major dictionaries to hand? Through the Internet you have these and many other reference works available. There are:

- word dictionaries

- rhyming dictionaries

- anagram machines

- thesauri

- translators, both human and computers.

Word dictionaries

Put the word 'dictionary' into a search engine and you could find 200,000 page references. There are specialist dictionaries for all subjects and all languages. You will never be short of the meaning of a word again! Oxford English and Webster are both available. Even better is Your Dictionary, a Web site that directs you to hundreds of dictionaries of all languages and descriptions at *www.yourdictionary.com*. Onelook Dictionaries (*www.onelook.com*) claims a word count of over 2,700,000 in 599 dictionaries, with more on the way, while at *www.dictionary.com* you will be given a 'word of the day'.

Writers' dictionaries

Reference dictionaries abound. Do you want a rhyme, to find out about a famous person from history or look up a phrase? They are all there.

There is a Rhyming Dictionary at *http://www.rhymezone.com/*. The Biographical Dictionary (*www.s9.com/biography*) has details of more than 27,000 notable people from ancient times to the present day. A Dictionary of Phrase and Fable is to be found at *www.bibliomania.com/Reference/PhraseAndFable/*.

Thesauri

There are far fewer thesauri than dictionaries, but Roget's is there at *www.thesaurus.com* in keyword-searchable form, just like a search engine.

The Getty Thesaurus of Geographic Names at *http//shiva.pub.getty.edu/tgn_browser/* is a geographical thesaurus, which will find every reference to a name around the world. Did you think that 'Thames' would only refer to London? Look it up here and be amazed.

The Wordsmyth Educational Dictionary and Thesaurus is an invaluable tool, offering 'various kinds of linguistic assistance and English language illumination'. It combines dictionary and thesaurus functions with powerful and flexible searching facilities. Find it at *www.wordsmyth.net/*.

Anagram machines

Have you ever wanted to work out anagrams for the names of famous people or places? There are plenty of sites to choose from, and they can be good fun as well as useful if you need an anagram.

You will find:

- Brendan's On-Line Anagram Generator (*www.mbhs.edu/~bconnell/anagrams.html*)

- The wordsmith site (*www.wordsmith.org/anagram/index.html*)

- Andy's anagram solver (*www.ssynth.co.uk/~gay/anagram.html*), which does it in English, French and Dutch.

TRANSLATORS

There are two types of translators on the Internet, Web-page-based and the human kind. They both give you translations of your text, but with differing degrees of accuracy. Here we take a quick look at both.

Translation web pages
The Internet can now translate your work automatically between various languages but with varying degrees of success. There is a serious problem with words that have multiple meanings, such as the word 'bat', when the hard, wooden kind might be suggested in the translation whereas the flying furry variety was what was needed. However, you can get a pretty good idea of what is meant.

Find them at *www.freetranslation.com* and *www.babelfish.com*. To use translation sites:

- either type some text into the Web page or supply a Web page address

- specify the translation required (e.g. Spanish to English) and click on the 'translate' button.

Human translators
If you need a piece of work translating, look no further than the Web. Directories of translators abound. There are translators' associations which offer search facilities to find members capable of doing your work, such as the American Translators Association (*www.atanet.org*).

Transref also offers a search facility to find translators by the criteria of your choosing, such as language, field of specialisation, country, etc. Their site is at *http://transref.org/default.asp?docsrc=/directory*.

On Line Translators (*www.infoteca.it/tradonline/eng/homepage_en.htm*) will translate between various languages and offer other text and language-based services.

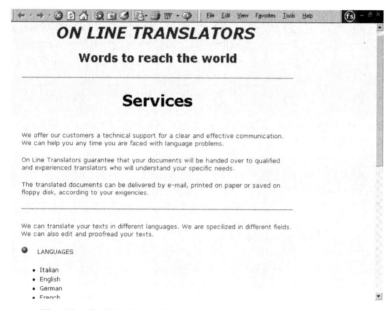

Fig. 15. On Line Translators' invitation to use their services.

A final word on what to search for

Go to any search engine and enter the words 'writers help'. You will be amazed by the number of sites you find, and the overwhelming generosity of the people who have put so much information on the Web for you to use. Add to that the commercial sites that aim to teach you (for a fee) how to improve your writing and you will never be short of help and guidance.

6

On-line Publishing

The Internet has been seen as a big opportunity for publishing. Some publishers use it for publicity. These are the book producers who want to spread the word about their wares, and encourage us to buy from the bookshop, either in person or on-line. Others see it as an opportunity to sell their publications direct, in electronic form, to the reader. No printing costs, no storage and no postage. Between these two extremes lie many other possibilities. How can we make the Web work to our advantage?

WHO'S ON LINE, WHAT DO THEY DO AND HOW DO I GET IN?

Conventional publishers

The quickest way to find a publisher's Web site is to enter the name in a search engine. Just the publisher's name will do. One of the first entries in the resulting index page will be the Web address. Go there and look for information on submissions. Another way is to try putting the publisher's name into a trial Web address. Try *www.howtobooks.co.uk*.

Remember, however, that just because you submit a book or article via a Web site or by email does not mean that it will be looked at any sooner. Have you tried to read an article on a computer? It isn't easy. Some first readers will take work home and sit with it wherever is most comfortable, and that probably does not include at a desk looking at a screen.

What you may find is the email address to which you should make your first contact, or a Web site giving details of what they want and how to submit it. You will be told if an email submission is permitted.

Electronic publishers

Electronic publishing is a new departure from conventional publishing. The problem it presents is how to collect the payment for the book or magazine you have published. So much of the material on the Internet is free that there is a marked reluctance on the part of readers to pay for information. However, **e-commerce** is growing in popularity and security, and now some credit card companies guarantee that you will not suffer from electronic fraud. There are two main areas of electronic publishing: on-line magazines (known as **e-zines**) and electronic books (or **e-books**).

E-zines

E-zines are electronic magazines, published on-line for readers to browse through, like web sites, or to download. They can also be sent to you by email, on a subscription basis. The beauty of the e-zine is that the reader can follow a link to a related site if something is found to be of interest. Once it is finished with it can be deleted without adding to the world's pile of scrap paper, or filed for future reference. Articles may be 'cut out' and filed.

Print-based magazines are following the Internet path by setting up Web sites. They often put extra articles and features on

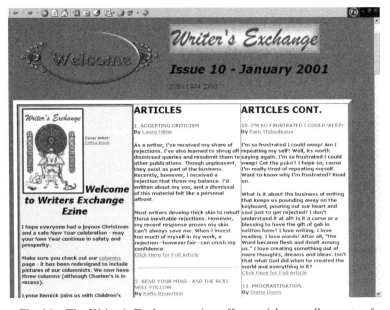

Fig. 16.   The Writer's Exchange e-zine offers articles on all aspects of interest to writers. It can be found at *www.writers-exchange.com/e-zine/current.htm.*

the Web site to encourage visitors to buy the magazine and to give magazine subscribers an extra area of interest when they are surfing the Web.

Where are they and what do they publish?
E-zines cover many subjects, writing-related matter included. Finding them is simple. Go to an e-zine listing site. Try going to Yahoo.com or Google.com and search for 'e-zine'. A recent search on Yahoo revealed over 1,000 sites. Google gave 50,000+ pages for the search 'e-zine', 7,000+ for 'e-zine writer' and 1,700+ for 'e-zine writer uk'.

A good e-zine for writers is **E-zee Writer** from **The Writers Bureau**. Its monthly offerings of writing-related articles can be found at *www.writersbureau.com/ezee.html*. Another useful e-zine is the **Writer's Exchange** (see Figure 16) and **Writers Store** will send you emails to tell you what is in their latest issue (*http://writersstore.com*).

E-books (electronic books)
E-books are books stored on computers ready for **downloading** over the Internet or for buying by post on **CD-ROM**. They may be stored on your computer or transferred into an **e-book reader** and they are supplied in varying **formats** depending on what equipment will be used to read them. They have many similarities to their printed cousins, such as 'cover' art work, illustrations, ISBNs and copyright clauses. They also have authors, editors and publishers.

The classic e-book must surely be the Encyclopaedia Britannica, which used to sell for upwards of a thousand pounds in print form and can now be bought for under £100 as CD-ROMS. As knowledge changes, links from the CD-ROM to the Britannica Web site (*www.britannica.co.uk*) keep the information up to date.

E-book readers
The e-book is a fairly new concept, and the technology for displaying it has taken a little while to catch up. Until recently you had to use a computer (desktop, notebook or hand-held) to read your e-book. At last, dedicated e-book readers are now coming on to the mass market in a range of types and prices, so that you no longer have to curl up with your PC to read one.

A number of manufacturers are starting to produce e-book

readers. The Franklin e-bookman, launched in late 2000, comes in a number of styles from around £120, with 8 to 16MB (megabytes) of memory, enough for something like eight to 16 books, depending on size. (One **byte** of memory stores one character on the page.)

The Rocket Ebook from NuvoMedia, see *www.rocket-ebook.com*, will store about 4,000 pages, expandable to 160,000. It weighs 22 oz., has a 4½" x 3" display and comes loaded with a dictionary. The Rocket is compatible with PC and Apple computers, which are used to download the books and transfer them to it. Thousands of free e-books are available for it from the company's library at *www.rocket-library.com*.

The SoftBook Reader is larger and heavier, weighing 2.9 lbs and with a 6" x 4" screen. It stores 5,000 to 50,000 pages and has a leather-like covering. Find out more at *www.softbook.com*.

Other e-book readers are expected from:

Compaq	*www.compaq.com*
Librius	*www.librius.com*
Psion	*www.psion.co.uk*
Palm Pilot	*www.palm.com*

Can I use my PC?

To read an e-book on a PC computer screen you need a program to convert the file into text and illustrations. It could be a Web browser or a purpose-designed reader program such as **Acrobat** from **Adobe**, which you can download free of charge from their Web site at *www.Adobe.com*. Many **shareware** program manuals are downloadable as Acrobat files. You can also use the **Glassbook Reader** program, also available free from *www.glassbook.com* and the **Everybook DocAble** program from *www.everybook.net*.

Acrobat uses files in **pdf** format. It is often preferred because the text retains the look of its original typography. It also allows annotations, bookmarks and other interactive features which make electronic books more interesting and useful than regular paper books. Other devices may also be used, such as Personal Digital Assistants (**PDAs**), i.e. pocket-sized computers used for note-taking and recordkeeping.

Different types of computer and reader need the book in different formats. The **Palm Pilot** hand-held computer from 3-Com needs the book to be in **Palmdoc** format, while Rocket e-book readers need the file in **HTML** format. This latter format may also be used to read books on any computer, using your Web browser.

Electronic book publishers produce books in all these formats. Books can be bought on-line for delivery by post on CD-ROM or may be downloaded over the Internet. The technology is growing in sophistication and user-friendliness, and is changing regularly. Hand-held readers are slowly coming down in price as they become more popular.

E-book publishers

As the technology improves and becomes more acceptable, so the number of e-book publishers grows. The biggest growth is in publishers of e-books accessed on-line, simply because there are no printing, postage and packing costs, unlike with CD-ROM distribution. Downloading from sites and transferring files as email attachments are the most cost-effective methods.

Why go to an e-publisher?
Traditional print-based publishers have a number of problems:

- handling bulky paper manuscripts
- the time it takes to get a book from manuscript to printed copy
- the storage space in the warehouse
- persuading bookshops to give you shelf space
- transporting the book to the shop
- further editions require more typesetting, printing and storage.

These problems simply don't exist for the e-publisher:

- The book is submitted electronically, on disk or by email.
- There is no typesetting.
- The book is stored with thousands of others on a computer disk.
- Customers buy direct, after browsing, via the Internet.
- The book is delivered by email, by downloading or on disk by post.

- New editions are simply mounted on the computer in place of the earlier edition.

The result is that authors can see their work available to the public much faster than it has been in the past. Books can be updated at little cost as soon as any information needs to be changed. Customers can afford more books and can keep them all for as long as they want without running out of shelf space.

The slowest part of the operation is the time it takes the editor to read and criticise the work (the only part of the task that cannot be automated) and this is taking longer as more and more authors submit their work for consideration. Some houses have to stop accepting submissions to stem the flow, so make sure that you check their Web sites before sending your work in.

What's in it for me?
Because it is such a new industry, the rewards for the writer vary enormously, from a proportion of the site's advertising revenue to a percentage of the monies taken by the book, anywhere from 10 to 70%, but typically 30 to 50%.

Rights also vary considerably, from the author retaining all rights in the work to the publisher retaining all rights, either for a fixed term or for the duration of the copyright life of the work. You must, therefore, check the contract thoroughly to see how much you are giving away. The National Writers' Association of America and the American Authors Guild have agreed contracts with some of the American publishers, but there are plenty around who are out to get as much as they can. Check your contract with the Society of Authors or another advisory body before agreeing to give your baby away. Recently in the Society's magazine, *The Author*, there has been a lot of correspondence and many articles on the subject of e-book contracts and copyright issues. Many e-publishers display their standard contracts on-line for you to download and inspect.

How do I submit my work?
Before you submit your work, look at other material on the site and see if you like it. Does your book fit in with other works they publish? If you can, contact the writers to find out how happy they are with the system. Also look to see how well the publisher advertises, both on and off the Web. It is no good having your book available if no-one knows it is there.

As with print publishers, submission methods vary from one company to another. Most prefer the text to be on disk or sent as an email attachment. To encourage this, some charge a fee for entering a paper manuscript into their system. Find out how your chosen publisher works by looking at the Web site. Most give submission guidelines on their sites and some will post you an information pack.

What will they publish?
Again, this depends on the publisher. Some offer to publish your out-of-print books, on the basis that if they were published commercially once, they could be successful again. Many have their preferred genres, as in print publishing.

Some publishers aim at the self-publishing market, selling you their expertise and assistance. Vanity publishers are also out there, but selling you their services at grossly inflated prices. Beware! Always check with a few companies before parting with your money!

Unpublished authors may be tempted to go to e-publishers for their first works. Some publishers will read and appraise books before taking them on. They want to make sure that they have a good chance of selling. Bookmice, at *www.bookmice.com*, offer such a service at no charge to the author. They guide you through all the steps and produce the book in a variety of formats. Their home page has links to submission guidelines, information for agents and resources for writers.

Authors Direct, at *www.wordwizard.com/indexbuy&sell.htm*, is a publisher with links to authors' Web sites and offers free Web space. They link up authors and readers, cutting out the middleman.

Allandale Online Publishing, at *www.allandale.co.uk*, want books on international relations and other political subject matter. They are academic rather than populist so no naughty ministerial exposés, please, and they pay 30%.

Netspace Publishing, of Carmarthen, Wales, at *www.netspace-publishing.co.uk*, appraise manuscripts and publish fiction which is up to their standard. They only ask for electronic rights for one year and the author keeps all other rights to sell elsewhere. There are no fees for holding books on their site and they do actively promote their wares. Unusually for an e-book publisher, the site for author submissions is totally separate from the book sales side, which is at *www.thebargainbookstore.co.uk*. Other e-publishers show both faces of their business on the one site. Royalties are a little over 30%.

AuthorsOnline, at *www.authorsonline.co.uk*, offer complete Internet expertise linked to publishing. They not only offer facilities to both new and established authors on a self-publishing basis but they also have links to print-based publishers to offer electronic versions of works in print. Another link will take you to suppliers of e-book readers.

Theirs is a total service using Internet technology to its fullest extent to take the book from author to reader. Writers are invited to submit books on disk, along with a CV, synopsis for the 'cover' and a two-line description for their index page. All should be on disk. They can scan typed manuscripts, but prefer not to.

There is no editorial input. This is a self-publishing organisation. They do, however, expect a high standard of English and will not entertain anything which might be considered illegal in the UK or in any country with which they have intellectual property rights agreements.

Authors have to sign a contract and return it with the disk and £49 for the service. The fee includes all publishing charges and the first year's hosting fee. Thereafter the book will be held on the Web site for an annual £10 payment. The contract includes permission to publish one chapter for free perusal by potential buyers (who like to browse). Authors receive 60% of the cover price.

A database is being established to link with other publishers' catalogues so that enquirers may locate both printed and electronic books in one search. Customers could then download e-books or order printed books direct. They are also offering e-book tokens, in denominations of £3, £10 and £20, for customers to buy as gifts. Visit the site or email *theeditor@authorsonline.co.uk* for an information pack.

And the traditional publishers?
Traditional print publishers Random House, Simon & Schuster and Time Warner have all started e-book departments. Others may follow their lead when they see the results of their experiences. Books will be published electronically on-line and also printed on demand so as to be available in bookstores. They will not be printed in bulk for distribution in the traditional manner.

Some traditional publishers are now digitising their printed books for electronic distribution. This is a good sign for the e-book trade as it shows that it is becoming more widely accepted.

7

Using On-line Archives and Information Services

WHAT ARE ON-LINE ARCHIVES?

On-line archives are articles from back numbers of newspapers and magazines, or research items on universities' and other organisations' computers, that have been stored electronically for reference. Many have been made available for access via the Internet, usually by means of Web browsers. More and more are going on-line all the time.

NEWSPAPER AND MAGAZINE ON-LINE ARCHIVES

Authoritative journals, usually broadsheet newspapers and more 'serious' magazines, that have an Internet presence are more likely to place selected articles and commentaries on-line for public access. The easiest way to find out if a journal has an on-line archive is to look for a reference to back number issues or search facilities on the home page. Some publications offer access to recent back issues while others allow searches going back years.

The Times (*www.the-times.co.uk*), the *Guardian* (*www.guardianunlimited.co.uk*), the *New York Times* (*www.nyt.com*) and the *International Herald Tribune* (*www.ht.com*) are just a few of the thousands of newspapers around the world that have Web sites. There are a number of sites that list on-line newspapers. Newspapers.com (*www.newspapers.com*) lists newspapers and magazines that have Web sites. It includes national, local and Web-only publications. See the appendix for a list of major publications that offer search facilities.

How do I access the information?

There is no standard way of finding archived information. There are some newspapers that allow browsing of articles from back issues, while others use search engines to help researchers find articles by entering key words. You may be offered the chance to enter dates between which you are looking for information.

Some journals offer free access to anyone, while others charge. Here are a few combinations of services:

- free browsing of recent back issues

- free access keyword searches and free viewing of articles

- free access keyword searches and viewing of synopses, payment per complete article viewed or downloaded

- free registration then free searches for registered users

- paid-for registration then free archive access.

Sometimes recent articles are free but older archives are charged for. Regular users may be able to run an account and be billed periodically, often at a discount. Casual users are asked to supply credit or debit card details.

This example shows how *The Times* (*www.the-times.co.uk*) allows free on-line searches of recent back issues. From their home page, the user clicks on 'Search' and sees the page shown below. The query or search term is entered in the box and the

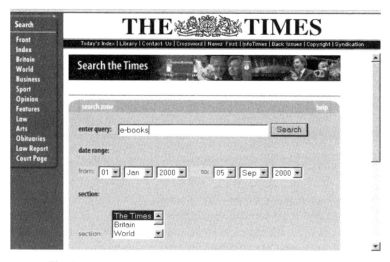

Fig. 17.   Looking for articles about e-books in *The Times*.
© Times Newspapers Ltd, London 2000.

'from' and 'to' dates are adjusted to the period to be covered. The section of the newspaper can also be narrowed down. Finally the 'Search' button is clicked on.

The results of the searches will vary in layout but they usually give the date of publication, headline, by-line and the first few lines or a résumé of the article. A hot link will take you to the article. If you want to use the article for research, save it on your computer and read it off-line later. This is far more efficient than reading it on-line. For any other use you should check the terms and conditions at the foot of the article or contact the Syndication Department of News International Newspapers on: *enquiries@nisyndication.com* (or the corresponding department of any other newspaper you have used).

Fig. 18.   Seven articles have been found; links to the first two
are shown.
© Times Newspapers Ltd, London 2000.

Searching a range of newspapers

If you want to search for recent news items on a certain subject, go to the News Index Web site (*www.newsindex.com*). There you can enter keywords to find articles from roughly 300 newspapers around the world.

UNIVERSITY ARCHIVES

Many universities store information electronically, mainly for use by their own staff and students. Some have free access but many require you to have a user name and password. To find out if you may use their services it is a good idea to email the university's librarian.

The COPAC service

The University of Manchester runs the COPAC service (*copac.ac.uk*), a 'one-stop shop' for accessing the merged catalogues of an increasing number of university libraries around the UK and Ireland. Three types of search are available:

- authors and titles
- periodical titles
- subject search.

To make a search, simply choose your search type, enter the details or key words and click on the 'Search' button.

The beauty of the system is in its ability to interrogate the catalogues of 19 libraries, listing the locations in which material is found. The results of your search can be emailed to you immediately, thus saving time printing out the results while you are on-line.

Although you cannot borrow books through COPAC, it is usually possible to borrow them from your local library by means of an inter-library loan. As the service grows, an increasing number of links to the texts are being provided, thus enabling you to read them on-line or to download them. If you are a member of a UK higher education institution you may well have permission to dig further into the COPAC members' libraries and access their materials on-line.

COPAC currently contains records from 19 catalogues, with four more being added. The list of participants includes the Universities of Birmingham, Cambridge, Durham, Edinburgh, Glasgow, London, Oxford and Southampton.

The libraries are all members of the Consortium of University Research Libraries (CURL) and the system is funded by the Joint Information Systems Committee (JISC at *www.jisc.ac.uk*).

Possible future developments include: letting potential borrowers know whether items are available, access to other (non-university) catalogues and searches of non-Roman script materials. More links to texts are planned and they are also working to improve accessibility to the COPAC Web site and interface for visually-impaired users.

Other universities world-wide

In order to discover other universities with on-line archives and research facilities you only have to do an Internet search. If you put the words 'university library on-line' into a search engine you will discover thousands of references. Many will be catalogues and indexes, some leading to on-line texts. Some universities also place their students' theses on-line.

Bath Information Data Services (BIDS)

BIDS provides on-line bibliographic databases for UK higher and further education establishments. Students or members of staff at UK academic institutions are the only authenticated users of BIDS. However, 'Ingenta Journals' is a BIDS service that can be free accessed at *www.ingenta.com.*

Individuals may register their details at this site to be able to search millions of articles from thousands of journals around the world. To make use of this service go to their Web site and click on 'Register'. You only need to leave your name and email address before starting to search free of charge.

When searching you will see brief details of the articles found, including the title, author, date and journal. If you find an article you want to see, you may supply credit card details for payment. You are told in advance how much an article will cost, and it may be in the region of £15 or more, but the searches are all free.

The Electronic Table of Contents (ZETOC)

If you want to find journal articles or conference proceedings, and you are a student at your local further education college or university, ask to use the ZETOC service (*http://zetoc.mimas.ac.uk*). It contains nearly 15 million articles from over 20,000 current journals and the titles of papers from around 70,000 volumes of conference proceedings. The search service is free but you may be asked to pay for copies of articles you request at the discretion of your college or university.

THE BRITISH LIBRARY

The largest collections of books in the UK are held in the British Library in London and Boston Spa, West Yorkshire. They offer free search facilities to the public, 24 hours a day, seven days a week (apart from occasional downtime for maintenance) on the British Library Public Catalogue site at *http://blpc.bl.uk*.

This new catalogue, which opened in January 2001, gives access to eight databases, comprising over 10 million bibliographic records, and includes the retrospective music file catalogue. There are books, patents, journals, conference reports and theses. All the databases may be covered in one search and an advanced search facility permits the full use of **Boolean operators** (the use of expressions 'and', 'or' and 'not', similar to the use of + and - with search engines).

Documents held at the London reading room may be inspected on the premises. Registered users may borrow items held at Boston Spa and photocopies may be purchased on-line. Full details can be found at *www.bl.uk/services/bsds/dsc/artdir01.html*.

The help system is context-sensitive all through the site, which makes it very user-friendly. Non-Roman characters are displayed in full.

The British National Bibliography (BNB)

At the time of writing, the BNB is available on the BLAISE Web site at *http://blaiseweb.bl.uk*, but it is due to be closed down. The BNB is available on CD-ROM and in printed form, and seven of the other BLAISE databases have been transferred to the BLPC (see above).

The remaining 12 databases are available either on CD-ROM or on-line, including through the Library of Congress database (*www.loc.gov*). Other bibliographic services may be accessed through the British Library's main Web site at *www.bl.uk* or the Library's ISP Web site at *www.britishlibrary.net*. Telephone help is available on 01937 546430.

8

Asking Questions

The presence of search engines on the Internet makes finding information easy, but the results do not always cover exactly what you might want to know. This is the time when you need to be able to find an expert and ask specific questions. The Internet has a large number of sites offering to answer your questions on a wide range of subjects.

The services are usually free and use email to deliver the answers. AllExperts at *www.allexperts.com* uses volunteer experts to answer questions, usually within a couple of days. On my nephew's behalf, I asked the question:

When did the Roman occupation of Britain end, why did they leave and who ruled the country after they had left?

When you visit the site you are asked to select a subject. I chose the 'Higher Education' link which includes History in its sub-heading. This led me to another menu of subjects, from which I selected General History. Then I was taken to a list of eight experts, each of them named with a brief resumé which indicated their areas of expertise.

When you select your expert you are shown more information about him/her and there is a link to 'Ask a question'. Click on this and you are asked for your name, email address, subject area and the question itself. After clicking on the 'Submit' button, you must state whether the response should be sent by ordinary email or sent 'priority' so that it goes straight to the top of your incoming mail list. Once this choice has been made, the question is sent direct to the expert, in this case a woman in New Zealand.

Once you have received your reply you may have follow-up questions. These can be sent to the same expert but some of them place a limit on the number of questions they are willing to take. It would be very easy for someone to overload an expert and they are doing it free of charge, after all.

RECEIVING THE ANSWER

Shortly after the question was sent I received an email confirming that it had been received. It also told me to expect an answer within three days.

Less than six hours later another email arrived giving me a hot link to click on to see the answer. Answers are available on the site for three days, after which they are removed.

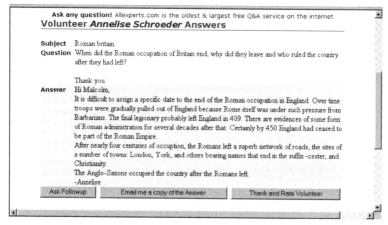

Fig. 19.   Response to my questions about Roman Britain.

Why do they do it? Simply because they are people who like to help others. The site is financed by advertising, but the experts are all volunteers. They come from all walks of life and include scientists, engineers, writers, teachers and scholars.

Other enquiry sites are available. I chose AllExperts simply because it was the first one I found and I was very happy with the results.

9

Radio Around the World

Radio broadcasting has always been a good source of material for those wanting to discover the facts of life abroad. Admittedly there is often a degree of propaganda from government-run broadcasting stations, but they do give a flavour of what life is like. Now radio has taken on a new dimension with the help of the Internet. Gone are the days of having to tune in to fading, distorted short-wave stations to hear about what is going on. Web-casting brings it all in loud and clear. There are even Web-only stations springing up.

WHAT CAN I HEAR?

The answer is 'almost anything you want'. There are tens of thousands of Web radio stations broadcasting music of all tastes, news and current affairs. The BBC broadcasts Radios 1, 2 and 4 plus some 5-live shows. The World Service is also there. Most mainstream radio stations are on the Web and independents are starting up all over the world. For other radio stations go to the Live Radio site at *www.live-radio.net* where you will find links to thousands of them from over 100 countries, or go to Web Radio at *www.web-radio.fm*. The sites have links to the stations and tell you which player software to use, RealPlayer or Media Player.

WHERE AND HOW CAN I HEAR IT?

The Live Radio site lists the radio stations, where they are based and what they broadcast – either live feeds or archived (recorded) programmes. The lists are split up into pages for Europe, USA, Canada, the rest of the world and net-only stations. Hobby stations are not included.

The links take you directly to the radio station and its live feed

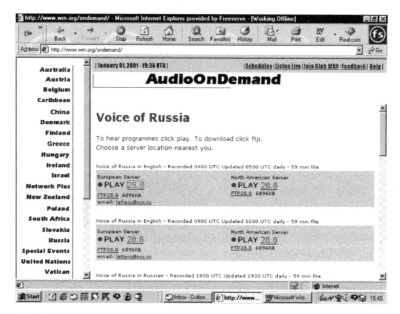

Fig. 20.   World Radio Network's link to Voice of Russia (*www.wrn.org*).
Click on PLAY and you will hear their English language news.

page. To hear the feed you must have previously loaded the **audio
stream** player software. The main software in use is RealPlayer,
which you may download free from *www.real.com/player*, and
Windows Media Player, from *www.microsoft.com/windows/
mediaplayer*.

Once the software is loaded, you can either go to one of the
Web radio link sites (see above) or type in the radio site's URL
direct. It will take up to a minute to connect and download the
audio stream. Then it will start playing.

One particularly informative station is Radio Nederland
Wereldomroep, based in Holland. Look for their site at
www.rnw.nl and click on 'On Air'. The standard of broadcasting is
excellent and it is informative on matters world-wide. They use
RealPlayer to broadcast. Email them at *letters@rnw.nl* and ask for
their twice-yearly newsletter called *On Target*.

For a range of links to broadcasters around the world, go to
www.wrn.org/ondemand/, the World Radio Network's link page
to 'on-demand' web radio sites. If you have the appropriate audio
streaming player program running, you will have the programmes
coming to you within a few seconds.

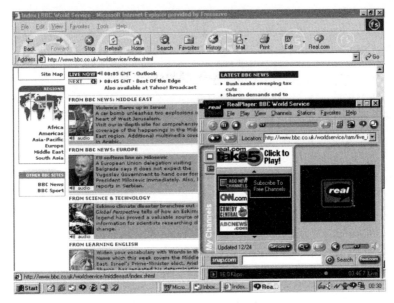

Fig. 21.   The BBC World Service
(*www.bbc.co.uk/worldservice/index.shtml*) broadcasts around the clock
on the Web. Note the URL in the RealPlayer location box.

10

Your Own Web Site

WHY HAVE A PERSONAL WEB SITE?

There are around 300 million Internet users world-wide. By the end of 2002 it is expected that there will be almost 500 million. Some 45% of them are in the United States. Having a presence on the World Wide Web is a cheap and effective publicity machine that is under your total control and which has an enormous potential audience. Write your story, display your CV and show everyone who visits your site just what you can do. If you are available as a writer, put up some examples of your work for everyone to see. You can then give your URL to potential publishers or clients rather than having to send them material.

There are some disadvantages. A Web site needs to be maintained and it can result in extra correspondence. Both are time-consuming but they are a small price to pay for the potential results.

There are four steps involved in setting up your Web site:

- Register your name.

- Design your Web site.

- Place your site with a hosting company.

- Enter your Web site URL in your account details at the registering company's Web site.

Once this is done, anyone who goes to *www.yourname.co.uk* will be redirected to your Web site, which will be hosted by your ISP. Although these are four separate steps, you will find that some companies will take care of most if not all the work involved.

REGISTERING YOUR NAME

A warning

Registering your **domain** name is vital! Your name is your first asset and point of contact, but there is nothing to stop other people registering your name and using it on the Internet.

Many famous and well-established writers have found that their names have been registered by others, known as **cybersquatters**, and money demanded for the domain registration to be handed over. The Society of Authors is looking after the interests of its members in this respect and is negotiating with various parties, but it is a drawn-out process. Far better to register your own name in the first place – it takes very little time and effort to do.

How to register

Look in any Internet-related magazine and you will find dozens of advertisements for name-registering companies. Some charge more than others, depending on the services they offer, but they all do the same thing. They take the name you want to use, check that it is available and register it for you with the naming authority.

This is what you do:

- Decide on the name you would like to use, with one or two alternatives in case your first choice is already in use.

- Go to a name-registering company's site, such as *http://oneandone.co.uk*.

- Type into the box the name you wish to register, e.g. *malcolmchisholm.co.uk*.

- Wait for the search to confirm that your name is available. If it has already been registered by someone else, try one of your alternatives.

- Supply your personal details for the registration and a password for future use.

- Supply a credit or debit card number to make the payment. The transaction is completed over a secure link, which reduces the risk of fraud to a minimum.

You now have your name registered and it is yours for two years. It must be renewed every two years, but the naming company should remind you in good time and simply charge you for renewal. No-one else can claim your name while you maintain the registration. It is important to register your name as soon as possible, otherwise someone else might get to it first.

In June 2001 I registered the name *malcolmchisholm.co.uk* with 1&1 Internet Ltd. The whole process took just 10 minutes and cost £11.38 including VAT. At the same time they automatically set up an account so that when I want to register another name or renew this one I simply enter the account number and password.

Once the process had been completed, the company sent me emails confirming that the domain name had been accepted by the naming authority, my account details and a VAT invoice stating the amount to be debited from my bank account. Don't forget to print the invoice and claim it against tax!

USING YOUR REGISTRATION

Email addresses

Once you have registered your name you can use it as an email address, irrespective of where you hold your regular email account. While your registration is maintained with the company, you can have emails redirected to the email account which you have with your ISP. You can put your new personal email address, such as *mail@mywebsite.co.uk*, on your letterheads, which looks more professional.

To set up the email redirection:

- Go to the registration company's Web site.

- Log on to your account with the username and password you set up when you registered your domain name.

- Enter the email name you want to use with your domain name, e.g. 'mail' or 'letters'.

- Enter the address to which you want the mail to be sent.

Once you have set up your domain name and email address, you can change the redirection address as often as you like, so that changing your ISP email address will be totally invisible to others and you do not have to send out change-of-address notifications.

Web site URLs

You will normally find that the registering company will offer you a Web redirection service. This allows you to publicise your personal URL. When it is accessed, the request for the page is redirected to your Web site at your ISP.

YOUR PERSONAL WEB SITE

While you are registering your name it is time to think about building your personal Web site. It is not difficult and there is a lot of help available. You can adopt a DIY approach, which is very cheap and fairly easy but a little time-consuming, or you can ask someone else to do it for you.

WHAT DO I PUT ON MY SITE?

Your Web site is there to sell you and your work. It has to make a good first impression and make the visitor want to see more. The opening page should introduce you with a short biography, picture and description of your work. Always bear in mind that new visitors to your site will decide in about ten seconds whether or not to continue looking, so immediacy is vital.

Your **home page** should open quickly and should show links around your site. Pictures are stored as separate files and these should be as small as possible to reduce the time taken for them to load. If, say, you write stories and poetry, keep examples on separate pages and show links to them plus an additional link to your full CV.

HOW DO I BULD MY WEB SITE?

A Web site is a collection of pages that contain hot links to take the viewer from one page to another. An example of a Web site may be as shown in Figure 22.

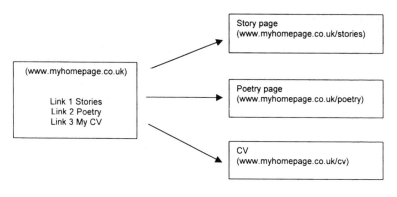

Fig. 22.

Plan for a simple web site

The visitor might arrive at the site by entering its URL. After seeing your home page they click on the appropriate link to view your stories, your poetry or your CV. Each of these pages should have a link back to your home page.

This is a simple example. You can place as many links on a page as you want. Each of your pages could show links to every other page on your site. You could show links to other Web sites, such as those of your publisher or the journals to which you already contribute.

Planning

It is vital to plan your site before you create any pages. Make sure that you do not leave anything out. Decide on what to include and what will be the best way to split it up. You could put everything on one page but that would take a long time to load and would be difficult to look round if your visitor is trying to find something in particular. Pages can be longer than the monitor screen but do not make them too big.

Your pages must be easy to read. Browsers display text in low resolution, which is tiring on the eyes. Make the most important points first, like newspapers do, to capture the reader's attention. Visitors will soon go elsewhere if you do not interest them quickly.

Decide on what external sites you want to link to. There may be other writers with whom you collaborate. They may want to link your site to theirs.

Page creation

Web pages are written in plain text. The special effects, such as italic or bold type, colours and pictures, are included by adding special instructions called **tags** to the text. This system is called **Hypertext Markup Language (HTML)** and it is very simple. It requires nothing more than a simple word processor or text editor. The pages are created as follows:

- Type the page using a word processor or text editor.

- Save the page in text form (i.e. not as a word-processed document).

- View the page with your Web browser.

Here is an example of a simple Web page. The page shown below has been generated by the text in Figure 24.

Note how the tags are used to switch on and off the bold, italic and underlined effects. Normally a word processor does these jobs transparently, i.e. you just switch the effects on and off. With HTML it is done by inserting tags. <B> switches bold on </B>

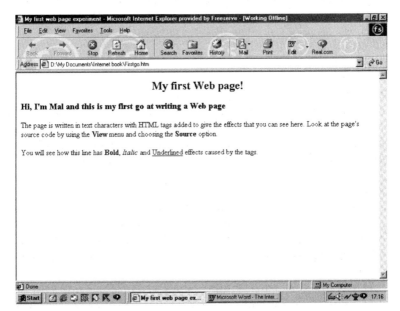

Fig. 23.   This is the result of viewing my test page with a Web browser.

```
<HTML>
<HEAD>

<TITLE>My first web page experiment</TITLE>

</HEAD>
<BODY>
<H2>
<CENTER>
My first Web page!
</CENTER>
</H2>

<H3>
Hi, I'm Mal and this is my first go at writing a
Web page
</H3>

The page is written in text characters with HTML
tags added to give the effects that you can see
here. Look at the page's source code by using the
<B> View </B> menu and choosing the <B>Source</B>
option.

<BR><BR>

You will see how this line has <B>Bold</B>,
<I>Italic</I> and <U>Underlined</U> effects caused
by the tags.
</BODY>
</HTML>
```

Fig. 24.

switches it off again. Line breaks are caused by the <BR> tag. The headings are created by <H2> and <H3> tags and the larger heading has been centred using the <CENTER> tag. (Note the American spelling.)

This is a fairly tedious way of creating Web pages. It can be done using either a word processor, such as Microsoft Word, or a simple text editor like Microsoft Notepad.

Using Microsoft Word

Go to the 'File' menu and choose 'New'.

Click on the 'Web pages' tab and select 'Web page wizard'. This will display a template Web page which you can edit using the

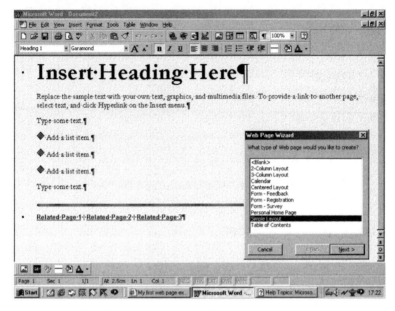

Fig. 25. Microsoft Word Web page template.

tools supplied. The help system can guide the novice user through the steps involved until you end up with a finished page.

The beauty of this method is that you can see the effects as you produce the page without having to use tags at all. It is, however, useful to know how tags work so that you can tweak them to make minor adjustments.

Find out about HTML by buying a specialist book (can be expensive) or going to a site which tells you how to do it (free). Sites such as Human Internet (*http://personalweb.about.com/ internet/personalweb/mbody.htm*) have enormous resources for the novice Web page builder.

Human Internet also has an email newsletter for Web designers, both novice and advanced, and an email discussion group to allow users to pick each other's brains when they have a problem. Go to the link 'Beginners Start Your Engines' for all you need to get started. Another link 'Personal Web Pages' takes you to pages about creating personal sites and shows you examples.

Web Reference, at *www.webreference.com*, is a site full of advice both for beginners and for advanced Web page writers.

They also have an email newsletter that you can subscribe to. It is delivered every few days with hints and tips to help you create better sites and pages.

MOUNTING YOUR WEB SITE

Your site is ready for the masses to visit. What do you do with it next? Your ISP will probably offer you some free Web space, anywhere from 5 to 20 megabytes, and this is usually good enough for a personal Web site. Your site is finished for the time being, although it will need maintaining as your work changes, but it is still sitting on your hard disk. How do you get it 'on air'?

File transfer protocol (ftp)

You may have noticed that Web site addresses begin with '**http**' This stands for hypertext transfer protocol and it is the means by which Web browsers **download** pages for display from **host** computers to terminal PCs. Passing pages in the other direction, from your terminal PC to the host, is called **uploading** and needs file transfer protocol (**ftp**).

Ftp software allows the terminal user to control the host computer, thus enabling a Web site operator at home to arrange pages on a Web site that has been mounted on a host. If you use Netscape Navigator as your Web browser, you can already use ftp, although it is limited in what it can do. A far more powerful program is **CuteFTP**, a shareware program available from *www.zdnet.com*. It takes a bit of setting up, but once it is done, it is a very effective program.

If you use an ISP to host your Web site, you will find that they offer you a file transfer program to use. It should already be configured to work with the ISP's Web site hosting system. This makes setting up much simpler because the host computer information will already be done for you.

Freeserve, for example, suggest that you use **TerrapinFTP**, supplied by Terrapin Internet Ltd. It is downloadable shareware and the licence costs £19.95. They are an English company, so if you don't like to use your plastic card over the Internet or the telephone you can post them a cheque. BTInternet, Freenetname, Global Internet and 24-7 Freecall also use Terrapin.

Downloading TerrapinFTP takes about 10 minutes. Unzipping the file is simplicity itself. (See the chapter on software for more details of downloading and unzipping files.) The first time I tried to upload a page took me 10 minutes, simply by following the instructions in their Web Wizard. The second time was much quicker. If all your pages are set up ready for the transfer, it takes only as long as the file transfer itself. The demonstration shown below took only five seconds once I had logged on to Freeserve. Larger, more complex pages will take longer.

Transferring your site to the host

For the purposes of this exercise, TerrapinFTP will be used as the example software.

Once your site is ready for transfer, make sure that it is all in one folder on your computer, and that you know exactly where it is on your hard disk. The page that will be seen first by visitors to your site is called the **home page** or **index page**. It will be called something like *index.htm, index.html, default.htm* or *default.html*, depending on the rules laid down by the host system that you will be using. Make sure that this is correct or you will never have any visitors.

Your Web site will be using a name such as *mywebsite.co.uk* or *mywebsite.myhostname.co.uk*. Again, this will have been arranged by your host system and should have been set up in your ftp software before you start to upload your Web site files. It you have everything in place, then start Terrapin.

In the following example, the site is made up of three pages: *index.html, template.html* and *textdemo.html*. They are saved in the folder D:\My Web Site. In order to transfer them to the host area on the Freeserve site they must be dragged to the site.

Look at the screen shot below. The host computer is shown in the upper half of the screen and the local computer in the lower half. The site currently contains two files, called *index.htm* and *index.html*. I want to replace them with the three new ones listed above. To transfer the files to the site, simply highlight them and 'drag and drop' them from the lower right area of the screen to the upper left area called *uploads.webspace.freeserve.net*. (This area has already been designated as the Web area in which your work will be displayed during the setup process.)

After the drag and drop has taken place, the existing *index.html* file will have been replaced by the new one. The two other new files will also be transferred to the host area. Terrapin also allows you to rearrange your Web site remotely from home. The

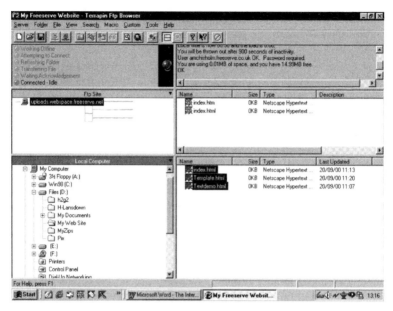

Fig. 26. Uploading Web pages using TerrapinFTP.

unwanted file, *index.htm*, was deleted by right-clicking on it with the mouse and selecting 'Delete'.

This is a very simple example. If your site is made up of folders and files, the operation is just the same, except that you drag the folder from the lower left corner of the screen straight up to the 'uploads' area. Remember, however, that if you have your site in a folder in the uploads area of the host, you must still have the initial index page in the uploads area and not in the site folder.

As you can see from the upper right corner of the screen, Freeserve allows users to have up to 15 MB of Web space, which is ample for most private users.

11

How the Internet Helps You to Sell

The fact that you are reading this book suggests that you want to write successfully. Part of the process is selling your work. After all, you don't just want to give it away, do you?

Selling your work successfully requires three different processes:

- market research
- contacting editors
- doing the writing.

The Internet makes the first two of these much easier. The third can also be helped with the abundance of help sites for writers which exist on the Web.

MARKET RESEARCH

This must be the most important work you do, apart from your actual writing. Whole books have been devoted to nothing else. If your work doesn't fit the magazine's audience or the publisher's list it simply will not sell into that market. Wrongly targeted work is the cause of up to 90% of rejections. How can the Internet help?

Most publishers of books and magazines have Web sites. Visit these sites and look. Find out what they sell and who buys it. If it is an e-zine, you will see the finished work on screen. If it is a printed magazine's Web site, some of the articles will be there to tempt visitors to buy. Naturally what is displayed will be aimed at the target audience. Book publishers (of both printed and e-books) will show their lists of publications. E-books will also show sample chapters to enable potential buyers to browse. These Web sites will also allow buyers to do subject-area searches. Do this yourself to see what is offered in your area of expertise.

If you cannot see recent issues of the magazines you want to research, you can still contact them and ask for submissions guidelines. Do it by email as a matter of course. The same applies to book publishers.

The fact that there are no national boundaries or distance barriers on the Internet makes it ideal for looking world-wide for outlets for your work. There are subject-based magazines in almost every country. How do you find them? With a search engine, naturally. Put in a search which includes the word magazine and the topic you are interested in. To limit the search to a country, include it in the search terms, e.g. to find a magazine about dogs in Canada, try:

$$+magazine +dogs +Canada$$

(Remember that the + signs insist that the words are included in the pages found.)

There are Web sites that list magazine titles. These are often international, based on countries. Use them to find Web site addresses. Use the Google search engine (*www.google.com*) to search for 'magazine publishers'. You will find magazines for almost every country in the world. It gave over 500,000 references when I tried this search.

Look out for sites which give help to writers. The Writers' Guidelines Database at *http://mav.net/guidelines* gives details of many paying markets. This site also pays for any items which it publishes.

CONTACTING EDITORS

Communication by email is very fast, enabling you to enquire anywhere about possible writing. Send the message now and you could have a reply from Australia tomorrow. Let this speed advantage help you. Assuming that an editor agrees to your proposal for an article, you can have the finished work emailed back very quickly. This puts you on the same footing as someone living in the country in which the publication originates. Editors plan ahead and have to work to deadlines. Using email to submit work helps to get it in on time.

One word of warning, however. Some American publications prefer to deal with people resident in the United States. Advertising your 'Britishness' with a *.co.uk* email address could be a disadvantage. Use a Yahoo.com or hotmail.com address, or register your own name as a *.com* domain name (e.g. *johnsmith.com*). It is perfectly acceptable and many writers do this.

DOING THE WRITING

The number of sites which offer help to writers is growing constantly. A lot of them are from educational sources, especially in the USA where many universities have creative writing courses, backed up by Internet Web sites. Refer to Chapter 5 for more information. A list of writers' help sites is in the appendix.

WRITERS WANTED!

What about looking for work on the Web? Just as there are writers looking for editors, so there are editors looking for writers. It does not matter where the writer is physically, as long as he or she is available and may be contacted. So when an editor needs a writer to do a job, an advertisement on a Web site can be seen by the whole Internet writers community.

Use a search engine to look for:

+writer +wanted +UK

and see what you get. The last search on Google.com revealed over 600 pages.

The list included advertisements for writers in residence, copywriters, comedy writers and many more. A few appointments were for 'virtual' posts, so-called because they could be carried out from anywhere in the world over the Internet. Some asked for volunteers, some were paid appointments. Without the '+UK' part of the search, over 70,000 pages were found. A good proportion offered payment.

Another search, for

+"technical writer" +english +wanted

revealed 2,850 pages. Again, a fair proportion were paid appointments, many of them freelance.

Most agencies and editors using the Internet to look for writers are based in America, but there is nothing to stop writers who live outside the US from applying. The number of European agencies doing the same is increasing (but, of course, US writers may apply here, too).

DO YOU KNOW A FOREIGN LANGUAGE?

Translation between languages is an ideal job to be done using the Internet. A text is emailed to the translator, who can have both the original document and the translation on-screen at the same time. The resulting translation is finally e-mailed back to the publisher. A search for

"translator wanted"

revealed 81,000+ pages. Without the quote marks, there were over a million.

COMPETITIONS

Many writers enter competitions. They are an interesting outlet, although not, of course, to be relied upon as a source of regular income. Use a search engine to look for

"+competition +writing" or "+competition +poetry"

for details of the many thousands of competitions organised by groups and societies around the world.

DON'T FORGET YOUR OWN WEB SITE

The previous chapter showed how to set this up, including:

1 your CV
2 your area/s of expertise
3 examples of your recent work.

Maintain the site by making sure that your recent work is current. It is no good showing examples of the kind of work that you don't want to do any more.

Make sure that anything you show, and which has already been accepted, is still yours to publish. Some publishers demand all rights, including electronic rights, thereby preventing you from showing your work on the Web.

When you contact an editor with a proposal, include details of your Web site, but only if it has something of worth to show. An editor won't be impressed by a site that doesn't show what you can do or have done in the past. A poor Web site will put people off.

12

Software – Programs to Help the Writer

So what software does a writer need? A word processor is enough surely? It aids the process of committing words to paper, so what more could you want?

As a writer you should be doing a lot more than just writing. How about planning your work? A good novel doesn't just leap out of the head and onto the keyboard. There are plots to unfold and characters to develop. If you write articles for a number of outlets, you need to track what is sent where. Nothing looks more unprofessional than sending the same article to a publisher twice, or even worse having the same piece appear in two different magazines. Laying out a play script is not easy, with its character names, speech, stage directions and comments.

All these tasks and more can be made easier with specialist software. It falls into four categories.

- story line developers
- layout assistants
- organisers
- tutoring systems.

STORY LINE DEVELOPMENT SYSTEMS

Do you have a story you want to write but have difficulty getting it to sound interesting? Could it be a real thriller but you don't have the ability to develop it? Story line developers help the writer by asking questions and suggesting threads for the plot. Some include stock situations into which the characters may be placed.

Templates are provided to create story plans or outlines. These contain many story elements to help build problems, characters and settings. There is help to find resolutions to the problems. Suggestions are made at each stage of development to aid the creative flow. Filling in the templates creates the outline ready for the writer to put into words. No more writer's block!

StoryBuilder from Seven Valleys Software (*www.svsoft.com*) is an example of a development system. They suggest that it 'lends structure to your premise, and helps build a solid foundation for your story'. It offers assistance with building the plot, characters and problems using 'tools for every aspect of story development'. It is definitely aimed at fiction writers. The Web site has snapshots of StoryBuilder to allow you to see how it works.

Another development tool, Dramatica (*www.dramatica.com*), from Screenplay Systems, aims to improve your work by encouraging you to 'focus on deep structure' by asking you questions. It is part of a suite of programs which includes Story View, a 'visual outliner', and Movie Magic Screenwriter, a scriptwriting word processor. You can download a demonstration version of Dramatica from the Web site.

The StoryCraft Web site (*www.writerspage.com/software.htm*) claims their system to be 'the world's most popular story-creation software'. It matches your story with one of 18 different patterns and gives you an outline to follow. Screen shots of a sample session may be viewed and it can be ordered on-line. A discount is available if you download as there is no disk to send and no postage and packing to be done.

The Literary Machine is a **shareware** program (see below) which helps to organise random thoughts and snippets of information. It is a customisable database for linking words and concepts. Download it from *http://sommestad.com/lm.htm*.

LAYOUT ASSISTANTS

The nature of play and screenplay scripts makes them tedious to create on a word processor. They include indentation, comments and directions, which require the use of a number of fonts. Dedicated word-processing software has been developed to simplify the task.

Scriptware from Cinovation Inc, (*www.scriptware.com*) is a full-featured word processor which is designed to do all the formatting work involved in scriptwriting for you. It automatically changes margins, sets capitalisation and does all the other time-consuming tasks required to lay out your script. Built-in formats include film, sitcom, play and dual-column audio/visual scripts. Formats for letters, memos, speeches, etc. are also included.

ScriptWright, from Indelible, Ink (*www.kois.com/ink/ swright.html*) is another script writing system, but it is an add-on for Microsoft Word. It supplies Word with all the styles and customisations needed to simplify the job of writing a script. A newsgroup exists for users to discuss matters related to ScriptWright and script writing at *news://www.kois.net*. The Web site offers technical support and FAQ pages. Also available are BookWright and PlayWright. Again, these are enhancements to Word.

Both the above sites offer free downloads of demonstration versions.

ORGANISERS

A busy writer will be constantly sending out new material and query letters. This needs to be tracked to make sure that it is not lying forgotten on an editor's desk, waiting on the writer's desk to be re-submitted or lying in the queue for re-working ready for a different market.

Ink Link (*www.inklinksoftware.com*) keeps the author informed about current submissions, submission histories, how much manuscripts have cost, how much they have earned, which markets are friendly and lots more. It is a complete recordkeeping system for all your manuscripts. They can be organised by date, title or subject. Financial reports can also be generated, ready for the day the tax form arrives.

The Working Writer is another writer's organiser. It can 'track the business of freelance writing from query letter to pay check'. The modules include document management, income and expenses, contacts, Internet links and date calculations. They are all easily inter-linked to allow the writer to fully customise the system. The system runs on Windows 3.1, 95, 98 and NT, and a Macintosh version is under development at the time of writing. A demonstration version may be downloaded from Dolphin Software's Web site at *http://dolphinsoftware.bc.ca/software/writers/*.

A shareware organiser called Writers Database is available for downloading at *www.netcomuk.co.uk/@0126fangorn/ultimathule*. It helps you to keep track of your manuscripts and build a database of proven and potential publishers.

TUTORING SYSTEMS

An alternative to the creative writing class, perhaps, is the Writer's Software Companion. See it at the Novation Web site (*www.novalearn.com*). It is a 'multimedia learning system for fiction writers' supplied on CD-ROM or it may be downloaded. It may be likened to 12 lectures on aspects of fiction writing, with exercises, examples, questions and answers. A cut-down version is available as a free download.

Creative Writing v2 from Way Ahead is a creative writing course which covers everything from writing fillers and readers' letters to poetry, stage plays, television and film scripts. The Web site at *www.hsc-ltd.demon.co.uk/wayahead* shows samples from various parts of the course.

SHAREWARE, CAREWARE AND FREEWARE

Some software developers take the view that potential users should be able to try before they buy. From this idea, **shareware** was born. Users can receive the software via any medium such as floppy disk, CD-ROM, email attachment or downloaded from a Web site. They are free to copy it and pass it on to others. Once they have tried it out they will either continue to use it or delete it from their computers.

If you try out shareware and decide to continue using it you are expected to pay for it in the form of a licence fee. The fee is payable to the copyright owner, who will register the fact that you have paid for it. When improvements are made to the software you will normally receive the updated version at no extra cost. A printed copy of the manual is often supplied when the licence fee has been paid.

The advantages of this system are:

- The developer does not have major advertising and distribution costs.

- Users recommend good software to others.

- Shareware libraries often supply CD-ROMs of related shareware so that users can try it and compare titles at very little initial cost.

- Users get good value for money.

It is, of course, the responsibility of the user to register with the supplier of the software, but it is all done on trust. No-one will know if you use the shareware without paying for it, but without the trust the system falls down and the supply of software will dry up.

In an attempt to make serious shareware users register, some shareware is distributed in a cut-down or demonstration form. Often some facilities are left out, for example, so that the work you do with it cannot be saved or it might not be able to print out your results. Sometimes the software will stop working after a period of time.

If you decide to pass shareware on to a friend, you must make sure that you pass it on in the form in which you received it, i.e. with all the files complete and with no alterations or additions. It is, after all, someone else's copyright material.

Dream Pack for Writers is a CD-ROM of shareware and freeware programs aimed at writers. It has been put together by Novation (*www.novalearn.com*) and contains 57 programs in 12 categories, which have been downloaded and tested by Novation.

Each program is supplied in the form of a self-extracting file. When you run it, it unzips and creates the files and folders needed for you to use it. Technical manual files are included for reference along with a link to the originator/author. Thus you can receive technical support and upgrades when necessary. The programs run on Windows 95, 98 or NT. See the details at *www.dreampack.com*.

Shareware libraries

Many Web sites include shareware libraries, from which you can download software or order it for delivery on disk. Downloading should cost you nothing apart from connection time on the phone. Be prepared to pay for someone to post you a disk.

Typical costs are from 50 pence to £2 for a floppy disk or up to £20 for a full CD. Bear in mind, however, that these are simply distribution costs. You may be expected to register your use of the software (see above) and pay accordingly.

Careware

Some shareware titles are distributed under the banner of **careware**. This is just the same as shareware, but some or all of the licence fee is paid to a good cause or a charity. The rules apply just the same, but in this case it is a charitable cause that's losing out when users don't pay the licence fee.

Freeware

Some software developers are generous enough to make their work available to others at no cost whatsoever, sometimes in the form of old versions of their work or software that has become obsolete. It is also a useful way for developers to have their new work tested, by allowing users to try it out free of charge and report back any faults or bugs they may find.

However, the same conditions apply to freeware as they do in shareware, in that it must be passed on to others in the same condition as you received it. Copyright rules still apply and the author must be given credit for the work, but it is not normally necessary for you to register your use of the material. Instruction manuals are usually in the form of a text file on the disk.

SquareNote version 3.5 is a freeware program which helps writers to collect, index, organise and retrieve their notes and ideas. The author describes it as 'computerised index cards, with automatic cross-referencing and indexing features'. It runs on any IBM-compatible PC under MS-DOS or Windows. Send an email to *sqn35net@sqn.com* for details or look it up at *http://sqn.com*. An advanced version is also available, but it costs $US 49.

A few points about downloading software and files

When you download software, it usually arrives in a compressed, or **zipped**, form. This allows it to arrive quicker, thereby saving download time and money, but it has to be unzipped before it can be used. Software is almost always delivered in the form of a self-extracting file. (See the section on downloading software with an example on page 128.)

Some software and many files are delivered in zipped form and need to be unzipped with a special program. There are a number of programs that will do this, the most popular being WinZip. Two versions are available: an evaluation version, which is share-ware, and a full commercial version. The advantage of the latter is that free upgrades are provided on the WinZip Web site (*www.winzip.com*) to keep it up to date.

WinZip is a useful program to have as it allows you to compress files and reduce their size by up to 50%. The advantages are:

- You can store much more data on your computer.

- The time taken to send files to others across the Internet is greatly reduced.

- You can archive much larger files onto floppy disk or more files onto a tape or zip drive.

Follow these steps to download the shareware version just to try it out:

1. Go to the Web site.
2. Click on 'Download Evaluation Version'.
3. Click on 'Download WinZip 8.0 for Windows'.
4. Click on 'Download now'.

The download takes a few minutes, but it is well worth the wait. Go to the appendix to see how to use WinZip.

It is not usually a good idea to compress files that you use regularly as it takes much longer to load and save them. If you are short of disk space, archive your old work onto floppy disks, tapes or CDs and remove them from your computer.

13

How to Create Word-Processed Documents from Web Page Material

Web pages are viewed using Web browser software. If you are using a Windows type of system where you can see more than one program running on the screen at a time, then you can copy items from the page in the Web browser window into a word processor. There are two types of operation:

- copying text
- copying images

COPYRIGHT WARNING!

Remember that everything you see on the Web has been put there by someone, and the copyright is still theirs even if it is free for you to view. Just because it is free to look at does not mean that it is in the public domain. Always obtain permission from the copyright holder before you start publishing anything you have found. Usually a polite email message is all it takes and I have never yet been refused permission.

HOW TO COPY TEXT

This is very simple:

- Place the mouse pointer at the beginning of the text to be copied.
- Hold down the mouse button and drag the pointer over the text to be copied so that it is highlighted.
- Press <CTRL> <C> to copy the text into the clipboard (i.e. hold down the key marked 'CTRL' and press the 'C' key).
- Open the document that is to receive the text.

- Press <CTRL> <V> to paste the text into the word-processed document.

Once the text is in the word-processor, you can edit it as normal. The only problem is that the page may be full of unwanted spaces and 'Return' characters which will need to be edited out. If the text surrounds an image, that might be copied and pasted at the same time.

HOW TO COPY AN IMAGE

Images should be saved to your computer's hard disk before they are imported into a document:

- Point at the image to be saved.
- Right-click the mouse.
- Click on 'Save picture as . . .' or 'Save image as . . .' from the menu.
- Save the picture.

Now go to the word processor document and place the image where you want it. If you are using Microsoft Word:

- Go to the 'Insert' menu and click on 'Picture'.
- Click on 'From file . . .'
- Use the dialogue box to choose the picture you saved. It will be inserted at the cursor.

14

Netiquette

The Internet is a free-and-easy place but there are some conventions that have grown up over time and established themselves as accepted behaviour. They are based on the notion that users should be considerate towards others.

EMAIL

- Always be brief and keep to the point. Email generates lots of traffic and people do not want to have to read long messages when a few words would do.

- Do not forward items to others unless you are sure that they would be interested. Never do it without the originator's consent. It is easy to do and can be tedious to receive.

- Do not attach large files for others to download, unless you are sure that they want or need them. It takes a lot of on-line time to download large files, so check with the recipient first.

- Advertising by email is called **spamming**. It is annoying to receive **spam** and sending out thousands of junk messages annoys thousands of people.

- Avoid the use of jargon unless you know the recipient will understand it.

- Never send abusive or derogatory messages to others. This is called **flaming** and you will get much worse back by return.

- NEVER WRITE USING ALL CAPITAL LETTERS. It is regarded as shouting. Use SPARINGLY for emphasis. You can also place **asterisks** either side of a word you wish to emphasise.

- Always remember that there are novices about who are learning the ropes as they go. Be forgiving of mistakes made by others.

'SMILEYS' AND ABBREVIATIONS

It is hard to express emotions in printed text, so 'smileys' or 'emoticons' have developed to help. They are simple combinations of characters which make up a facial expression. View them sideways.

:-) happy	:-(sad
;-) winking	:-o surprised
8-) smile from wearer of glasses	:-D big smile
:-V shouting	:-# I'm saying nothing

Abbreviations are used to express commonly used sayings. It is part of the informality of emailing, which is also expressed in the frequent use of first names to address people you do not know.

BTW By the way	IMO In my opinion
FWIW For what it's worth	IMHO In my humble opinion
FYI For your information	IOW In other words
OTOH On the other hand	RTFM Read the flipping manual
TIA Thank you in advance	WRT With regard to

FREQUENTLY ASKED QUESTIONS (FAQS)

When you are asking for information always remember to read the FAQ list or page first.

Internet people are very generous of their time, but there are so many newcomers that those in the know are often overloaded. To overcome this problem, lists of questions that have been asked many times before are published. You will usually find that your problems are solved by consulting the FAQ list.

If you do not find the answer then by all means ask the expert, but remember that he or she is probably busy and has taken time out especially to help you. Some FAQ pages are so large and comprehensive that a search engine is incorporated to help you find the answers.

15

Take Care, Now!

It is a sad fact of life that there are many people who take delight in causing problems for others. This is no less a problem on the Internet. You will find:

- viruses

- hoaxes

- frauds

- chain letters

- anonymous sources

- pornography.

VIRUSES

A virus is a computer program that has been written to attack other people's computer files. There are thousands of them, from simple ones that cause minor inconvenience to really nasty, vicious ones that will wipe out all your files. A number of them were written by bored, Eastern European programmers as a form of retribution against their masters when they were not being paid. Others were written by teenagers just to be awkward, a form of mindless computer vandalism.

They are usually transferred from one computer to another by attaching themselves to files saved on disks. When an infected file is loaded into another computer, the virus copies itself on to other files, thus spreading to more computers when files are shared with other people.

Some viruses spread by attaching themselves to email messages and activating when the attached message is read. More recent viruses do not even have to have their messages opened and read. They automatically run as soon as they arrive.

The latest viruses can also be embedded in the code of Web pages. They activate when you simply look at a page.

A virus will be designed to attack a particular computer or program. It cannot spread from one design of computer to another, i.e. an Apple computer will not catch a virus from an IBM PC and vice versa.

How can I protect myself?

There are anti-virus programs that will check your computer for viruses regularly. They are loaded with the details of all known viruses and they check the computer memory and disks when the machine is switched on. They also check any file on a floppy disk or CD-ROM when it is loaded. If any viruses are discovered, a warning message is given and, depending which virus it is, it may be removed.

Make sure that you install one of these programs. (Some experts suggest that since most anti-virus systems only catch 95% of viruses, you should install two.) There are plenty available. They may be bought from computer suppliers, computer bookshops and by mail order. It is also important to keep the list of viruses that your program checks for up to date. Users are invited to register their purchases to enable them to receive updates as they are issued, usually from a Web site. The cost of updates is included in the purchase price and is valid for a year or more, depending on the supplier.

The following anti-virus programs are all effective:

Software	Web site http://
Dr Solomon's Home Guard	www.drsolomon.com
Inoculan	www.cheyenne.com/virusinfo/
McAfee Virus Scan	www.mcafee.com
Norton Anti-virus	www.symantec.com
Quarterdeck ViruSweep	www.quarterdeck.com
Sophos Inter-Check	www.sophos.com

Is there anything else I can do?
You can reduce your risk by taking some sensible precautions:

- Never open an email attachment from someone that you do not know and trust.

- Always let the anti-virus software check your computer completely before you attempt to use it.

- Always check a disk that has been in someone else's computer. They may not know that they have been infected. (To check a floppy disk, put it in the disk drive and click on it to view its contents, or run your anti-virus scan on the floppy disk drive.)

Email viruses
Email programs are often subject to virus attack. The viruses spread by mailing themselves to all the addresses in the mail program's address book. Once installed on a machine they then move to the address book and repeat the process the next time the user goes on-line.

When you hear of a virus it will soon be followed by a software revision to close the loophole, thereby preventing an attack. It is a good idea to go to the software manufacturer's Web site and download the latest version.

Information on viruses is passed on in newsgroups. Look at the following:

- *alt.comp.virus*

- *comp.virus.*

HOAXES

Following on from, and related to, viruses are hoax emails. They are perpetrated by people who think it is fun to cause upset and chaos by spreading false information. Emails can be sent hundreds at a time for very little cost. So people can easily spread rumours and misinformation very quickly.

An example was the 'Good Times' hoax, which was an email sent to dozens of people warning of a virus. They were asked to pass the message on to all their friends in order to do them a favour. The result was that millions of email messages were clogging up mail server computers and people were receiving dozens of copies of the same hoax warning.

FRAUDS

Emails are often anonymous because of the way the system runs. Only honest folk put their names and addresses at the end of their messages. Thus it is easy to make fraudulent claims by email without being caught. Beware of messages claiming that you will receive thousands of pounds if you send money or messages to others. Remember that if an offer seems too good to be true, then it usually is.

CHAIN LETTERS

For many years chain letters have been sent by post, requesting that you send money to an address and send the letter on to four more people. Bad luck is supposed to result if you break the chain.

The same is happening by email, causing a lot of unnecessary traffic and upsetting people who are superstitious. Remember, these messages are created by unscrupulous people who care nothing for the feelings of others. They either hope to cause disruption to others or make a quick profit out of other people's fears. Do not reply to them. Simply delete the message and forget about them. Nothing will happen to you as a result of your actions.

ANONYMOUS SOURCES

As you have probably realised, the Internet is the ideal way to send out anonymous information. Take these steps when using the Net:

- When you receive an email message from a source you do not recognise, treat it with suspicion.

- Chat room correspondents may not be honest about who or what they are. Never agree to meet someone for the first time alone. Parents should be careful to check their children's chat room contacts and conversations. Paedophiles are using them more and more to entrap children.

- Never agree to sign a contract with, or send money to, a site that does not give a verifiable postal address and telephone number. Someone who wants to do genuine business will always give references.

- Be aware that anyone can set up a Web site and say whatever they want.

- Always check information you read on an unknown Web site. Anyone can display anything, true or false, and claim it is authentic.

PORNOGRAPHY

There is an enormous amount of pornography on the World Wide Web. The people who put it there go to great lengths to get round the blocks put up by ISPs who want to prevent its spread. Some innocuous searches can reveal unpleasant sites and there is some-times no warning at all when you click on a hot link.

ISPs monitor the sites that their clients visit and police forces monitor the activities of known porn sites in order to see who visits them. It is illegal to send porn across public networks and anyone caught doing so is liable to an embarrassing prosecution. Employers with Internet connections to their corporate networks put up blocks on known porn sites and regularly record the Internet activities of their employees.

The home-office user does not necessarily have the facilities to prevent others in the household from visiting where they will, so many ISPs have a 'Family Friendly' setting to prevent children from accessing porn. It is usually password protected.

Finally, it is illegal to keep certain pornographic images on any computer, so it is important to make sure that no-one else has access to your Internet connection and hard disk. Keep your dial-up software settings protected by a password.

APPENDICES

Internet Service Providers

FREE ISPS

ISP (and parent company)	Contact	Web address
Egg (Prudential Banking)	0345 233233	www.egg.com
Freeserve (Dixons)	CD from Dixons	www.freeserve.co.uk
Ic24 (MGN group)	0870 9090 262	www.ic24.co.uk
LineOne	0800 111210	www.lineone.net
Netscape (AOL)	0800 923 0009	www.netscape.com
PowerGen	0870 606 0653	www.powergen.co.uk
Sainsbury's	CD from stores	www.sainsbury.co.uk
Tesco	CD from stores	www.tesco.co.uk
UK online	0800 053 4500	www.ukonline.net
Virgin Net	0500 558800	www.virgin.net

PAID FOR SERVICES

Paid-for Internet access is sold as being more reliable, with the addition of specialist services only available to subscribers. There may be some free on-line time included. Here are a few providers:

ISP	Contact	Monthly access fee
AOL *www.aol.co.uk*	0800 376 4444	Various rates and on-line charges
BTInternet *www.btinternet.com*	0800 800 001	£9.99 or £14.99 depending on access times
Claranet *www.clara.net*	0845 355 1000	£5.99 includes some free Internet access call time
Compuserve *www.compuserve.com*	0870 6000 800	£7.50 plus locall call charge
Gemsoft *www.gemsoft.net*	0114 275 7070	£12.99
Global Internet *www.global.net.uk*	0870 909 8041	£29.99 + VAT per quarter
Pipex dial *www.pipex.net*	0500 474 739	£12.75 + VAT + £11.50 set-up fee
Sonnet Internet	020 7891 2000	£12.50 plus local call charge
Which? Online	08459 830240	£14.75 + £11.75 set-up fee

*Some paid-for services give you a one-month free trial. Prices are liable to change, so check with the ISPs before making a decision.

Email Address-Finding Services

These services provide email address-finding facilities and some also hold telephone numbers and postal addresses:

Four11 Directory Services	*www.four11.com*
WhoWhere?	*www.whowhere.com*
LookUP!	*www.lookup.com*
Internet Address Finder	*www.iaf.net*
InfoSpace	*www.accumail.com/iui/index.htm*
Lycos	*www.whowhere.lycos.com/Email*
NetPages	*www.aldea.com/wwwindex.html*
InterNIC X.500 Directory Services	*www.internec.net/ds/dspgx500.html*
Yahoo	*www.yahoo.com/docs/family/more.html*

Newspapers and Magazines Offering News and Search Facilities

Thousands of newspapers have an Internet presence. Put the title you want into a search engine to find it. These are a few newspapers from around the world with useful facilities.

Name	Web site	Type of searches and charges
The Australian	*www.theaustralian.com.au*	Recent reports on Australian themes free. Links to other newspapers
The Guardian and *The Observer*	*www.guardianunlimited.co.uk/ Archive*	Keyword and date searches, articles free
Japan Times	*www.japantimes.co.jp*	Free search back to April 200 under development
Le Monde Interactif	*www.lemonde.fr/service/0,232 1,109-QUO,00.html*	Free searches and articles back to 1987
The New York Times	*www.nytimes.com*	Free searches of recent articles News sent by email
The New Zealand Herald Online	*www.nzherald.co.nz*	Keyword searches and articles free
Reuters	*www.reuters.com*	International news
Russia Today	*www.russiatoday.com*	News by email from East European newspapers and *China Today*

Seattle Post-Intelligencer	*seattlep-i.com/archives*	Keyword search free, articles CAN$1.95
The Straits Times Online	*straitstimes.asia1.com.sg*	Keyword searches for recent articles free
The Times and *Sunday Times*	*www.the-times.co.uk*	Keyword search, recent articles free
The Times of India	*www.timesofindia.com*	Indian national and regional news
The Wall Street Journal	*interactive.wsj.com*	Paid subscription for services then free keyword searches, articles US$2.95, headline news free
The Washington Post	*www.washingtonpost.com*	Keyword search free, articles US$1.50 or $2.95
Die Welt	*www.welt.de*	Keyword searches and reports free

Payment is usually made by credit or debit card, by entering the details into a form on a secure Web page, along with your name and address for delivery.

On-line Writing Laboratories (OWLS)

University	OWL address
Dakota State University OWL	*www.departments.dsu.edu/owl/default.htm*
University of Illinois Writers' Workshop	*www.english.uiuc.edu/cws/wworkshop/ index.htm*
University of Maine Writing Center	*www.ume.maine.edu/~wcenter/welcome.html*
Massey University (NZ) OWLL	*owll.massey.ac.nz/*
University of Michigan OWL	*www.umich.edu/~nesta/OWL/owl.html*
University of Missouri Online Writery	*www.missouri.edu/~wleric/writery.html*
Purdue University OWL	*owl.english.purdue.edu*
Rensselaer Writing Center Online Handouts	*www.rpi.edu/dept/llc/writecenter/web/ handouts.html*
St Cloud State University, The Write Place	*leo.stcloudstate.edu*
University of Surrey English Language Institute	*www.surrey.ac.uk/ELI/welcome.html*
Temple University Writing Center	*www.temple.edu/writingctr/cweb500.htm*
University of Wisconsin Madison Writing Center	*www.wisc.edu/writing/handbook/main.html*

Expert Question Sites

These sites offer the chance to ask questions of scholars and experts. Select the subject, ask the question and wait for the answer, usually within a few days or maybe within hours.

Site	Address
AllExperts	*www.allexperts.com*
Ask a Librarian (UK public reference libraries, factual queries only, cannot research answers)	*www.earl.org.uk/ask*
Ask-A-Question	*www.ipl.org/ref/QUE*
Ask an Expert	*www.askanexpert.com*
Askme.com	*www.askme.com*
AskTony	*www.asktony.com*
ExpertCentral.com	*www.expertcentral.com*
Expert Search	*www.expertsearch.co.uk*
InformationOutpost	*www.informationoutpost.com*
Net Query (for Internet-based questions)	*www.bbc.co.uk/webwise/query*
The Virtual Reference Desk	*www.vrd.org*

Useful Addresses
(on the Web, of course!)

Arts Council of:
> England: *www.artscouncil.org.uk.*
> Email: enquiries@artscouncil.org.uk. Tel: 020 7333 0100.
> Wales: *www.ccc-acw.org.uk.*
> Email: information@ccc-acw.org.uk. Tel: 01222 221447.
> Ireland: *www.artscouncil.ie.* Email: info@artscouncil.ie.
> Tel: 00353 1 6761302.
> Scottish Arts Council: *www.sac.org.uk.*
> Email: help.desk.sac@artsfb.org.uk. Tel: 0131 240 2443.

American Library Association. *www.ala.org.* Email: ala@ala.org.
> Tel: 001 202 628 8410.

Arvon Foundation. *www.arvonfoundation.org.*
> Email: bank@arvonfoundation.org. Tel: 01422 843714.

Association of British Science Writers. *www.absw.org.uk.*
> Email: absw@absw.org.uk. Tel: 020 7439 1205.

Association of Freelance Journalists.
> *members.tripod.co.uk/AFJ_2/AFJ_2-2.*
> E-mail: afj_uk@yahoo.com.

Association of Investigative Journalists. *www.aij-uk.com.*
> Email: aij@aij-uk.com. Tel: 0709 121 6085.

Author.co.uk. *www.author.co.uk.*

Authors Licensing and Collecting Society. *www.alcs.co.uk.*
> Email: alcs@alcs.co.uk. Tel: 020 7395 0600.

AuthorsOnLine. *www.authorsonline.co.uk.*
> Email: theeditor@authorsonline.co.uk. Tel: 01992 503151.

Book Trust. *www.booktrust.org.uk.*
> Email: booktrust@dial.pipex.com. Tel: 020 8516 2977.

British Science Fiction Association. *members.aol.com/tamaranth.*
> Email: bsfa@enterprise.net. Tel: 01327 361661.

British Guild of Travel Writers.
> *ourworld.compuserve.com/homepages/BGTW/homepage.htm.*
> Email: bgtw@garlandintl.co.uk. Tel: 020 7720 9009.

British Library. *www.bl.uk*. Email: britishlibrary-net@bl.uk.
Tel: 01937 546060.

Federation of Worker Writers & Community Publishers.
www.fwwcp.mcmail.com. Email: fwwcp@cwcom.net.
Tel: 01782 822327.

Institute of Journalists. *www.ioj.co.uk*.
Email: memberservices@ioj.co.uk. Tel: 020 7252 1187.

National Association of Writers Groups.
www.author.co.uk/nawg. Email: mikediane@tesco.net.
Tel: 01262 609228.

National Association of Writers in Education. *www.nawe.co.uk*.
www.artscape.org.uk. Email: paul@nawe.co.uk.
Tel: 01653 618429.

Poetry Society. *www.poetrysoc.com*. Email: info@poetrysoc.com.
Tel: 020 7420 9880.

Publishing Training Centre at Book House.
www.train4publishing.co.uk.
Email: publishing.training@bookhouse.co.uk.
Tel: 020 8874 2718.

Romantic Novelists Association.
homepages.poptel.org.uk/wendywoo/rna/table_index.html.
Email: see web site.

Society of Authors. *www.writers.org.uk/society*.
Email: authorsoc@writers.org.uk. Tel: 020 7373 6642.

Society of Indexers. *www.socind.demon.co.uk/*.
Email: admin@socind.demon.co.uk. Tel: 0114 281 3060.

Society of Women Writers & Journalists.
www.author.co.uk/swwj.html. Email: swwriters@aol.com.
Tel: 01444 416866.

trAce on-line writing community. *trace.ntu.ac.uk*.
Email: trace@ntu.ac.uk. Tel: 0115 848 6360.

Writers' Exchange. *owl.wsu.edu/shared.asp*.
Email: ljohnson@mail.wsu.edu.

Writers' Guidelines Database. *mav.net/guidelines/*.
Email: guidelines@mav.net.

WinZip – How To Get It and How To Use It

Archiving your work is vitally important to you as a writer. Zipping up the files means you can fit more onto a floppy disk or tape drive. Downloading software always makes use of zipped files to reduce the transmission time. WinZip is the most popular file compression system in use. This section tells you how to download and set up WinZip ready for use.

DOWNLOADING WINZIP

Follow these steps to download the shareware version in order to try it out. Once the file has been downloaded you will be asked where to store the file. Agree with the suggested location.

1. Go to the Web site *www.winzip.com* and follow these hot links:
2. Click on 'Download Evaluation Version'.
3. Click on 'Download WinZip 8.0 for Windows'.
4. Click on 'Download now'.

After a few minutes the software will have downloaded.

UNZIPPING AND SETTING UP WINZIP

The next step is to unzip the file and extract the program files. The Setup software will do it for you but you will have to give it a helping hand. At various points in the process Setup will ask you to confirm where the software is to be stored on your hard disk. Accept the suggestions made by WinZip. They are the best choices and you would only want to change them if you had a special reason to. Most users will find them satisfactory.

Now it is time to run the SetUp program:

- Click on the 'Start' button.

- Click on 'Run . . .'

- Enter 'C:\Program Files\winzip80.exe' in the box and click 'OK'.

- In the WinZip8.0 Setup box click on the 'Setup' button.

- Setup will suggest installing the software in the folder C:\Program Files\WinZip. Accept this choice by clicking on 'OK'.

- When Setup has installed the program, read the information box and click on 'Next'.

- Read the licence agreement. Note that you have 21 days in which to try out WinZip, after which must pay $US29 or uninstall the software. (You can pay by Visa on their secure Web site.) Click 'Yes' to agree to the conditions.

- Read the features list box. Click 'Next'.

- Print the Quick Start guide. Click 'Next'.

- Because you are new to WinZip, select the WinZip Wizard, which will guide you through zipping and unzipping files. Click 'Next'.

- Allow WinZip to search through your hard disk for folders containing zipped files. Click 'Next'.

- Click 'Next' without selecting the 'Association' box.

Finally the WinZip folder appears. It shows you which programs and files have been installed. You will see:

- the on-line manual

- a 'What's New' text file, giving the latest developments

- a 'Read-me' text file which gives installation details

- the WinZip program

- the Uninstall program which helps you to remove the program if you decide not to keep it.

WinZip should also have been installed on your 'Start' menu, so that you can run it quickly when you click on the 'Start' button.

USING WINZIP

Now WinZip is ready for use. It is a good idea to try it out with a file which is safely saved and also backed up onto another medium. Here is how to zip up a file and save it to a floppy disk in drive A:

Zipping up a file

- Click the 'Start' button. On the start menu click on WinZip.

- If you have not registered your software, click on 'I agree'.

- In the WinZip Wizard Welcome box click 'Next'.

- Select 'Create a new zip file' and click 'Next'.

- In the Choose Zip Name box enter the name of the Zip file you want to create. To create a file on drive A: called Fred, type 'A:\Fred' and click 'Next'.

- Now you have to indicate which files are to be compressed and put into A:\Fred. Click on 'Add files . . .'. Select a file to be zipped up and click 'OK'. Repeat this as often as necessary. When you are ready click 'Zip Now'.

- If you want to create another Zip file click 'Next'.

- If you want to email the file to someone else click 'Mail this zip file . . .'.

- If you have finished, click 'Close'.

Now look at the Zip file you have created and compare it with the combined sizes of the files you have zipped up. You should find a significant saving in disk space.

Once you are used to the system, you may care to use the 'Classic' screens rather than the Wizard:

- Click on 'New' to start a new archive file.

- Enter the name of the file and select its folder or drive in the dialogue box.

Fig. 27.   Enter the archive file name in the dialogue box.

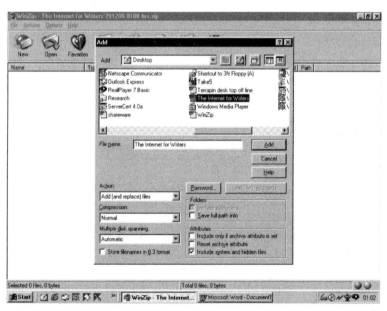

Fig. 28.   Use the 'Add' dialogue box to select files for achiving.

- Select the files to place in the archive in the 'Add' dialogue box.

- Follow the directions to insert more disks if more than one is needed.

- The summary of the archive file will be displayed.

Unzipping files

When you want to restore zipped files:

- Run WinZip and agree to the terms.

- In the WinZip welcome box click 'Next'.

- In the 'Select Activity; box select 'Unzip or install from an existing zip file'. Click 'Next'.

- In the 'Select Zip File' box click on 'Search . . .', select 'Search disk:', choose drive A: and click 'OK'. Now click on 'Next'.

- In the 'Unzip' box select the folder you wish to restore the files to, or accept the default supplied. Click 'Next'.

- The unzipped (or restored) files will be displayed in a folder, ready to be moved to where you want them or to be processed.

Remember that a zipped archive file will contain the data present when you archived it. Do not restore it back to the directory or folder where you keep the working copy. This will overwrite the later version with the earlier one and your later work will be lost. WinZip will normally offer to restore files to a new folder inside the 'Unzipped' folder. This new folder will have the same name as the zip file you are restoring.

BACK UP YOUR FILES FOR SECURITY

Keep regular backups of your current work. You never can tell when your hard disk will fail, your computer will be stolen or the office will catch fire. For ultimate security, important work should be archived to at least two backup disks or tapes and one copy should be kept away from your premises.

Internet backup services

You may like to keep backups or archives on servers dedicated to that purpose. Freedrive (*www.freedrive.com*) is a file storage service that offers up to 50 megabytes of free storage for your files. The service is advertised as a 'Free Internet Hard Drive'.

Users may upload files for storage or for sharing with others. If they are needed, simply download them once more. If the files have been zipped up, the storage volume available is increased considerably, maybe by up to 50%, depending on the compression ratio (ratio of zipped size to normal size).

Users sign on over a secure link (like the links used for banking services) and save their files in a password-protected area. They may then retrieve the files from anywhere in the world. Other suggestions are for group sharing of files and for family sharing such as with holiday photographs. One group member uploads the files to the archive and other family or group members can then download them.

FilesAnywhere (*www.filesanywhere.com*) offers a similar service.

Self-Extracting Zipped Files

A lot of downloaded **applications software** comes in the form of self-extracting files. When you download software *always* save it in a known location on your hard disk before unzipping or using it. You have already seen how to download WinZip and the same principles apply to all downloaded, zipped software.

Self-extracting files will normally be saved in your program files area on your hard disk. To set them up, run the self-extracting program and it will tell you where the application software will be saved. You will normally be given a suggestion as to where to save it, and it is usually a good idea to accept the suggestion. Only save it somewhere else if you know exactly what you are doing and you have a very good reason for doing so.

There are two stages to obtaining software from the Internet:

- Download it.
- Install it.

The comments in italics indicate what happens when installing 'The Working Writer'.

DOWNLOADING THE SOFTWARE

- Go to the site you wish to download from and find the required file(s). (*http://dolphinsoftware.bc.ca/software/writer*).
- Click on the download link on the Web page.
- When asked, tell the program to save it to disk.
- Accept the suggested location for saving the program file and make a note of where it has been saved, usually in the program files folder (*C:\Program Files*).

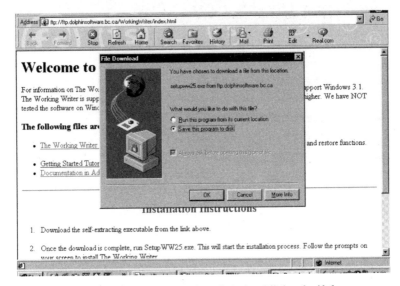

Fig. 29.   The Working Writer download link asks if the
file is to be saved.

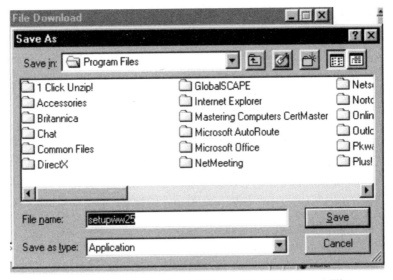

Fig. 30.   Saving the downloaded file to drive C:\Program Files.

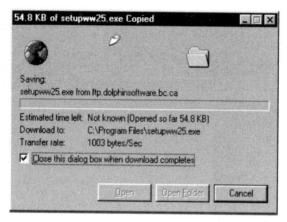

Fig. 31. Monitoring the progress of the download operation.

When the download is complete (you can monitor its progress on the screen) close the Internet connection unless you need it for something else.

INSTALLING THE SOFTWARE

- Make sure that you are not running any other application during this process.

- Run the Setup or Install file which you downloaded (*C:\Program Files\setupww25.exe*).

- Accept the location that the Setup program suggests for saving the files (*C:\Program Files\Working Writer*).

- Accept any default settings for the software unless you have a good reason for changing them.

- Wait for the Setup/Install process to be completed.

The software is now ready for use.

There is no standard means of running the software once it has been installed. Working Writer places a launch icon on the desktop screen to enable you to run it immediately. WinZip places an entry in the start menu, so you can run it after clicking the Start button.

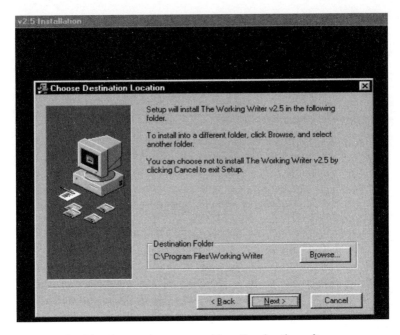

Fig. 32.   Accept the suggested location for the software.

Shareware will normally have a manual written for it. It may be included in the downloaded zipped file or it may be a separate download. The Working Writer's manual is a downloadable **pdf** file (i.e. a file readable with **Acrobat** document reader software). Sometimes a printed manual is provided when you register the use of the software with the supplier.

Country Codes and Domain Names

There are currently 245 codes representing countries on the Internet. They show where the domains have been registered, but the pages and sites are not necessarily located there. Domains registered in the USA do not have a country code. Instead they have a 'top level domain name code' that indicates the type of organisation that has registered. A selection is shown here. A full list can be found on *www.workz.com/content/401.asp*.

AD = Andorra
AT = Austria
AU = Australia
BE = Belgium
BG = Bulgaria
BR = Brazil
CA = Canada
CH = Switzerland
CN = China
CS = Czechoslovakia (former)
CY = Cyprus
CZ = Czech Republic
DE = Germany
DK = Denmark
EC = Ecuador
ES = Spain
EU = Europe
FI = Finland
FR = France
FX = France, Metropolitan
GB = Great Britain (UK)
GI = Gibraltar
GL = Greenland
HK = Hong Kong

HU = Hungary
ID = Indonesia
IE = Ireland
IL = Israel
IN = India
IQ = Iraq
IR = Iran
IS = Iceland
IT = Italy
JP = Japan
LI = Liechtenstein
LU = Luxembourg
MC = Monaco
MO = Macau
MT = Malta
MX = Mexico
MY = Malaysia
NL = Netherlands
NO = Norway
NZ = New Zealand
OM = Oman
PE = Peru
PH = Phillippines
PK = Pakistan
PL = Poland
PT = Portugal
RO = Romania

RU = Russia
SE = Sweden
SG = Singapore
TR = Turkey
TW = Taiwan
UA = Ukraine
UK = United Kingdom
US = United States
VA = Vatican City State (Holy See)
YU = Yugoslavia
ZA = South Africa
COM = US Commercial
EDU = US Educational
GOV = US Government
INT = International
MIL = US Military
NET = Network
ORG = Non-Profit Organisation
ARPA = Arpanet
NATO = Nato

Glossary

Acrobat. Software used for reading text files, included in electronic book readers and computers.

Adobe. Suppliers of Acrobat document reader software.

Address book. List of email addresses used with email software, can include phone numbers and postal addresses for reference.

ADSL. Asymmetric Digital Subscriber Line, for permanent high speed connection to the Internet.

Applications software. Programs which do work for the computer user, e.g. word processor, database, diary and organiser.

ASCII. American Standard Code for Information Interchange. Code used for transmitting and storing text on computers. Also used to describe text-only documents.

Audio stream. Sound broadcast through the Internet for you to hear using a sound card and audio software.

Baud rate. Speed at which your modem receives data, measured in bits per second. Modern modems work at up to 56,000 bps (56kbps).

Book mark. Web page URL stored in a browser file to enable the user to return to it at a later date.

BT Openworld. BT ISP that uses the ADSL system.

Byte. Computer memory needed to store one character of text.

Cable modem. Modem used to link a computer to a cable telephone system, much faster than a normal modem.

Careware. Shareware programs whose licence fee helps good causes.

CD-ROM. Compact disk used to store or distribute programs and data.

Chat room. Web page used to enable visitors to 'chat' by text messages.

.co. Commercial Internet domain, also used for personal names, e.g. bbc.co.uk.

.com. American/international commercial Internet domain, e.g. bt.com.

Conference. Two or more people using an Internet page or connection at the same time to exchange information.

CuteFTP. Shareware program for transferring files between computers.

Cybersquatter. Someone who registers another person's name on the Internet and demands money for its release.

Data. Electronic information.

Data transfer rate. Speed at which data is transmitted over a link, measured in bits per second (bps).

Deja news. Search engine used to find newsgroup information.

Desktop. The computer screen on which all icons and work areas are displayed.

Desktop conferencing. Two or more people using a common link to work jointly with software and data.

Domain. Area of the Internet owned or shared by users.

Domain name. Name registered by a domain user.

Download. Transfer data from a host computer to one which has logged on to that host.

Drag or **drag and drop**. The action of selecting files on the screen desktop and moving them to another part of the desktop with the mouse pointer.

E-book. A book stored as a computer file rather than on paper. It is read using an e-book reader.

E-book reader. Hand-held computer used to store and read an e-book, or a computer program used to read an e-book on a desktop computer.

E-commerce. Buying goods and services over the Internet using credit/debit cards for payment.

Electronic book (e-book). A book stored as a computer file rather than on paper. It is read using an e-book reader.

Electronic mail (or email). Messages sent from one computer to another via the Internet.

Emoticon (or smiley). Facial expression made up from text characters in an email message to show emotion.

Everybook DocAble. E-book reader program.

E-zines. Electronic magazines viewed by Web browsers over the Internet. Usually no printed version.

FAQ. Frequently-asked questions in a list for novices to check before asking questions of others.

File attachment. A file sent by email is 'attached' to the message.

Firewall. Software that prevents unauthorised access from the Internet into a network.

Format, file format. The way in which a file is stored on disk. The format used depends on the software that uses it.

Freeware. Software that is free of charge.

ftp. File transfer protocol, means for uploading data.

Glassbook. E-book reader software.

Hard copy. A copy that is printed on paper.

Header. Line repeated at the top of every page of a document.

Home Highway. BT's high-speed digital telephone system using ISDN technology.

Home page. The first page you come to on a Web site or the page your Web browser goes to when it starts.

Host. Large computer to which others log on in order to connect to the Internet.

Hot links. Highlighted text or images which, when clicked on, lead the reader to another page.

Hypertext Markup Language (HTML). Language used to write Web pages.

Hypertext transfer protocol (http). System used to transfer web pages from one computer to another over the Internet.

Icon. A small image on the computer screen which performs a task when it is clicked on.

Index page. List of pages resulting from a search on a search engine.

Internet. The world wide network which links computer networks.

Internet access provider. Commercial provider of Internet access to smaller users but without any information content.

Internet Service Provider (ISP). Commercial provider of Internet service to smaller users, also providing own information content.

ISDN. Integrated Services Digital Network, the digital phone and computer network.

Launch icon. An icon on the desk top which may be double-clicked to start a program.

Log in or **log on**. Link your computer to a host computer such as an ISP.

Mainframe. Large computer used by large company or government, often as powerful as thousands of PCs.

Megabytes of RAM. Size of Random Access Memory in a computer (the more, the better) measured in millions of characters of space.

Microsoft Internet Explorer. Web browser program supplied by Microsoft.

Microsoft Outlook Express. Email handling program supplied by Microsoft.

Modem. Device used to connect a computer to a telephone line to enable the user to contact other computer systems.

.net. Internet domain name element indicating an organisation that is connected with the operation of the Internet or plays a major part in it.

Net, the. Abbreviation for the Internet.

Netiquette. Unwritten rules that govern what is or is not acceptable behaviour on the Internet.

Netscape Communicator, Netscape Navigator. Web browser programs supplied by Netscape Communications Corporation.

Netscape Messenger. Email and newsreader program supplied by Netscape.

Newsgroup. Group of linked news messages on a particular theme.

Newsreader. Program used to read Usenet news messages.

Off-line. Not connected to a host computer.

On-line. Connected to a host computer.

.org. Internet domain name element indicating a non-profit organisation.

Outbox. Location in an email program where messages wait until they are sent to the recipients.

OWL, On-line Writing Laboratory. A Web site devoted to helping writers improve their techniques.

Palmdoc file. A file used by Palm Pilot hand-held computers.

Palm Pilot. A type of small, hand-held computer.

Password. A word known only to a user for security reasons, it must be typed in to gain access to a computer system.

PC. Personal computer.

PC-compatible. Made to run in the same way as an IBM PC.

pdf. Type of file used to read electronic books on PCs and electronic book readers.

Pentium 75. IBM-compatible computer, slow by today's standards.

Plain text. Text with no formatting such as bold or italic.

Posted. Displayed on the Internet, esp. mail and news messages.

Protocol. A set of rules that governs how data is transferred from one computer to another.

Public domain software. Software that is free of copyright restrictions and may be freely used and copied.

RAM. Random Access Memory, used to run programs in a

computer. More memory means more programs can be run at the same time or the computer can run faster.

Real time. When what you have on your computer is happening at the same time as the event which is sending the information, such as viewing live webcam pictures.

Rocket Ebook. A hand-held device used to read e-books.

Search engine. Computer that searches out relevant pages of information connected to words supplied to it.

Serial port. Connector on a computer used to link to a modem, called a COM port on a PC.

Service provider. Organisation that provides a connection to the Internet, via telephone lines.

Shareware. Software that may be freely copied and distributed to others (but if you decide to use it you should register its use with the author and pay a fee).

Smiley (or **emoticon**). Facial expression made out of text characters in an email message to show emotion.

Snail mail. Emailers' name for the postal system.

SoftBook Reader. A hand-held device used to read e-books.

Software. Computer programs.

Spam. 'Junk' email messages used to advertise.

Start button. Windows button at the bottom left corner of the desktop. Click on it to run your programs and to shut down the computer.

Start menu. The menu that appears when the 'Start' button is clicked.

Status bar. At the bottom of a browser screen, shows what proportion of a Web page has been received.

Surf the Web. Explore the World Wide Web.

Tag. Code placed in a Web page to create an effect or a hot link to another page.

TerrapinFTP. Downloadable shareware program.

Thread. A series of email or news messages with a common theme.

Toolbar. A row of screen icons in an application program such as a word processor or Web browser which may be clicked on.

Topic headings. Links on a search engine to frequently-used areas of information.

Uniform resource locator (url). Address used to find Web resources, also known as a Web address.

Unmetered. Phone calls which are untimed – only a single fee is paid irrespective of how long you maintain the connection.

Upload. Transfer data from a computer to a host computer.

Url. Uniform resource locator, used to find Web resources, also known as a Web address.

Unsent mail folder. Location in an email program where messages wait until they are sent to the recipients.

Usenet news. Email-like messages posted to newsgroups for all to read.

User ID. User identification used to log in to a computer system, usually in conjunction with a password.

WAP. Wireless Access Protocol. The system of getting Web pages onto mobile phone screens.

Web address. Address to enter into a Web browser to reach a Web page.

Web browser. Program used to look at Web pages.

Web cam. A camera showing live pictures on a Web page.

Web pages. Pages of information reachable on the Web.

Windows. Windows 95 and 98 operating systems by Microsoft, which run your computer and allow you access to programs.

Wizards. Systems which help users to install new software and configure their computers.

World Wide Web. World wide network of computers that store Web pages.

www. Prefix to most World Wide Web page addresses.

WWW. Abbreviation for the World Wide Web.

Zipped. Compressed so that it takes less time to download or copy.

Further Reading

MAGAZINES

These UK magazines are listed in alphabetical order. They are all good, so visit their Web sites and see which ones you like the look of.

. net   www.netmag.co.uk
Future Publishing, 30 Monmouth Street, Bath BA1 2BW. Tel: 01225 442244. Fax: 01225 732282. Email: paul.douglas@futurenet.co.uk.

Internet Advisor   www.netadvisor.co.uk
Future Publishing. Tel: 01225 442244. Fax: 01225 732282.

Internet Magazine   www.internet-magazine.com
Angel House, 338-346 Goswell Road, London EC1V 7QP. Tel: 0845 601 2672. Fax: 01858 435 958. Email: tanyak@internet.emap.com

Practical Internet   http://binky.paragon.co.uk/pi/
Paragon Publishing, Paragon House, St Peter's Road, Bournemouth BH1 2JS. Tel: 01202 299900. Fax: 01202 299955. Email: mnewman@paragon.co.uk.

The Internet Mole   www.molemag.net
PO Box 329, Bury St Edmunds IP31 3EZ. Email: mole@molemag.net.

EZINES

Author.co.uk   www.author.co.uk
Email: ezine@author.co.uk. Tel: 01394 273388.

E-ZEE WRITER   www.writersbureau.com/ezee.html
Email: ezeewriter@writersbureau.com.

Writers Exchange   www.writers-exchange.com/ezine.current.htm

Writers Store   http://writersstore.com
Email: news@writersstore.com.

Index